PRENTICE HALL

SCIENCE EXPLORER

Astronomy

Prentice
Hall

Needham, Massachusetts
Upper Saddle River, New Jersey
Glenview, Illinois

PRENTICE HALL
SCIENCE EXPLORER

Astronomy

Book-Specific Resources

Student Edition
Annotated Teacher's Edition
Teaching Resources with Color Transparencies
Consumable and Nonconsumable Materials Kits
Guided Reading Audio CDs
Guided Reading Audiotapes
Guided Reading and Study Workbook
Guided Reading and Study Workbook, Teacher's Edition
Lab Activity Videotapes
Science Explorer Videotapes
Science Explorer Web Site at **www.phschool.com**

Program-Wide Resources

Computer Test Bank Book with CD-ROM
How to Assess Student Work
How to Manage Instruction in the Block
Inquiry Skills Activity Book
Integrated Science Laboratory Manual
Integrated Science Laboratory Manual, Teacher's Edition
Interactive Student Tutorial CD-ROM
Prentice Hall Interdisciplinary Explorations
Probeware Lab Manual
Product Testing Activities by Consumer Reports™
Program Planning Guide
Reading in the Content Area with Literature Connections
Resource Pro® CD-ROM (Teaching Resources on CD-ROM)
Science Explorer Videodiscs
Standardized Test Preparation Book
Student-Centered Science Activity Books
Teacher's ELL Handbook: Strategies for English Language Learners

Spanish Resources

Spanish Student Edition
Spanish Guided Reading Audio CDs with Section Summaries
Spanish Guided Reading Audiotapes with Section Summaries
Spanish Science Explorer Videotapes

Science Explorer Student Editions

From Bacteria to Plants

Animals

Cells and Heredity

Human Biology and Health

Environmental Science

Inside Earth

Earth's Changing Surface

Earth's Waters

Weather and Climate

Astronomy

Chemical Building Blocks

Chemical Interactions

Motion, Forces, and Energy

Electricity and Magnetism

Sound and Light

Acknowledgments ·····························

Activity on page 37 is from *Exploring Planets in the Classroom.* Copyright by Hawaii Space Grant Consortium, based on a concept developed by Dale Olive. Essay on page 129, copyright ©1995 by Valerie Ambroise. All rights reserved. Used by permission.

ISBN 0-13-054088-9
2 3 4 5 6 7 8 9 10   04 03 02

Cover: This photo of Saturn and three of its moons is a montage of images taken by NASA's *Voyager 1.*

Program Authors

Michael J. Padilla, Ph.D.
Professor
Department of Science Education
University of Georgia
Athens, Georgia

Michael Padilla is a leader in middle school science education. He has served as an editor and elected officer for the National Science Teachers Association. He has been principal investigator of several National Science Foundation and Eisenhower grants and served as a writer of the National Science Education Standards.

As lead author of *Science Explorer,* Mike has inspired the team in developing a program that meets the needs of middle grades students, promotes science inquiry, and is aligned with the National Science Education Standards.

Ioannis Miaoulis, Ph.D.
Dean of Engineering
College of Engineering
Tufts University
Medford, Massachusetts

Martha Cyr, Ph.D.
Director, Engineering
   Educational Outreach
College of Engineering
Tufts University
Medford, Massachusetts

Science Explorer was created in collaboration with the College of Engineering at Tufts University. Tufts has an extensive engineering outreach program that uses engineering design and construction to excite and motivate students and teachers in science and technology education.

Faculty from Tufts University participated in the development of *Science Explorer* chapter projects, reviewed the student books for content accuracy, and helped coordinate field testing.

CHAPTER PROJECT

Book Author

Jay M. Pasachoff, Ph.D.
Professor of Astronomy
Williams College
Williamstown, Massachusetts

Contributing Writers

W. Russell Blake, Ph.D.
Planetarium Director
Plymouth Community Intermediate School
Plymouth, Massachusetts

Thomas R. Wellnitz
Science Teacher
The Paideia School
Atlanta, Georgia

Reading Consultant

Bonnie B. Armbruster, Ph.D.
Department of Curriculum
   and Instruction
University of Illinois
Champaign, Illinois

Interdisciplinary Consultant

Heidi Hayes Jacobs, Ed.D.
Teacher's College
Columbia University
New York, New York

Safety Consultants

W. H. Breazeale, Ph.D.
Department of Chemistry
College of Charleston
Charleston, South Carolina

Ruth Hathaway, Ph.D.
Hathaway Consulting
Cape Girardeau, Missouri

Teacher Reviewers

Stephanie Anderson
Sierra Vista Junior
    High School
Canyon Country, California

John W. Anson
Mesa Intermediate School
Palmdale, California

Pamela Arline
Lake Taylor Middle School
Norfolk, Virginia

Lynn Beason
College Station Jr. High School
College Station, Texas

Richard Bothmer
Hollis School District
Hollis, New Hampshire

Jeffrey C. Callister
Newburgh Free Academy
Newburgh, New York

Judy D'Albert
Harvard Day School
Corona Del Mar, California

Betty Scott Dean
Guilford County Schools
McLeansville, North Carolina

Sarah C. Duff
Baltimore City Public Schools
Baltimore, Maryland

Melody Law Ewey
Holmes Junior High School
Davis, California

Sherry L. Fisher
Lake Zurich Middle
    School North
Lake Zurich, Illinois

Melissa Gibbons
Fort Worth ISD
Fort Worth, Texas

Debra J. Goodding
Kraemer Middle School
Placentia, California

Jack Grande
Weber Middle School
Port Washington, New York

Steve Hills
Riverside Middle School
Grand Rapids, Michigan

Carol Ann Lionello
Kraemer Middle School
Placentia, California

Jaime A. Morales
Henry T. Gage Middle School
Huntington Park, California

Patsy Partin
Cameron Middle School
Nashville, Tennessee

Deedra H. Robinson
Newport News Public Schools
Newport News, Virginia

Bonnie Scott
Clack Middle School
Abilene, Texas

Charles M. Sears
Belzer Middle School
Indianapolis, Indiana

Barbara M. Strange
Ferndale Middle School
High Point, North Carolina

Jackie Louise Ulfig
Ford Middle School
Allen, Texas

Kathy Usina
Belzer Middle School
Indianapolis, Indiana

Heidi M. von Oetinger
L'Anse Creuse Public School
Harrison Township, Michigan

Pam Watson
Hill Country Middle School
Austin, Texas

Activity Field Testers

Nicki Bibbo
Russell Street School
Littleton, Massachusetts

Connie Boone
Fletcher Middle School
Jacksonville Beach, Florida

Rose-Marie Botting
Broward County
    School District
Fort Lauderdale, Florida

Colleen Campos
Laredo Middle School
Aurora, Colorado

Elizabeth Chait
W. L. Chenery Middle School
Belmont, Massachusetts

Holly Estes
Hale Middle School
Stow, Massachusetts

Laura Hapgood
Plymouth Community
    Intermediate School
Plymouth, Massachusetts

Sandra M. Harris
Winman Junior High School
Warwick, Rhode Island

Jason Ho
Walter Reed Middle School
Los Angeles, California

Joanne Jackson
Winman Junior High School
Warwick, Rhode Island

Mary F. Lavin
Plymouth Community
    Intermediate School
Plymouth, Massachusetts

James MacNeil, Ph.D.
Concord Public Schools
Concord, Massachusetts

Lauren Magruder
St. Michael's Country
    Day School
Newport, Rhode Island

Jeanne Maurand
Glen Urquhart School
Beverly Farms, Massachusetts

Warren Phillips
Plymouth Community
    Intermediate School
Plymouth, Massachusetts

Carol Pirtle
Hale Middle School
Stow, Massachusetts

Kathleen M. Poe
Kirby-Smith Middle School
Jacksonville, Florida

Cynthia B. Pope
Ruffner Middle School
Norfolk, Virginia

Anne Scammell
Geneva Middle School
Geneva, New York

Karen Riley Sievers
Callanan Middle School
Des Moines, Iowa

David M. Smith
Howard A. Eyer Middle School
Macungie, Pennsylvania

Derek Strohschneider
Plymouth Community
    Intermediate School
Plymouth, Massachusetts

Sallie Teames
Rosemont Middle School
Fort Worth, Texas

Gene Vitale
Parkland Middle School
McHenry, Illinois

Zenovia Young
Meyer Levin Junior
    High School (IS 285)
Brooklyn, New York

Contents

Astronomy

Activities

Searching for the home of
COMETS

It's a long way from astronomer Jane Luu's office in the Netherlands to the mountaintop in Hawaii where she searches the night sky. But astronomers need dark skies, far from city lights. They also need clean, clear air to see deep into the solar system. That's why Jane Luu travels all the way to the high mountain observatory in Hawaii. Jane Luu has traveled long distances before. Born in Vietnam, she came to the United States at the age of 12.

"As a kid in Vietnam," she says, "I didn't have a single class in science. But after studying physics in college, I got a job at the Jet Propulsion Laboratory, the place where they track all the unmanned space missions. It was a summer job, pretty unimportant stuff. But when I saw the pictures taken by *Voyager I* and *Voyager II* in the mid-1980s, I thought they were spectacular. Those pictures of the planets were what made me go to graduate school in planetary astronomy."

Object in the Kuiper Belt

Dr. Jane Luu
arrived in the United States from Vietnam as a young girl. Dr. Luu studied physics at Stanford University in California and astronomy at the Massachusetts Institute of Technology. She now works at Leiden University in the Netherlands.

TALKING WITH DR. JANE LUU

What Jane Luu looks at now lies just beyond the farthest planets in our solar system. It's a ring made of millions of ice-rock pieces that circle the sun. Luu and her co-worker David Jewitt first discovered these objects in 1992. The rocky planet Pluto is the biggest object in this ring—called the Kuiper (KY pur) Belt. Pluto travels through space along with an estimated 30,000 other objects that Luu and Jewitt have named "Plutinos" (little Plutos). Objects in the Kuiper Belt sometimes escape from the belt and approach the sun. The sun's heat then makes them light up and become comets.

Q *Why did you start searching for the Kuiper Belt?*

A There were two reasons. We wanted to know if there was anything beyond Neptune besides Pluto. Why should that space be empty when there were so many planets and smaller objects nearer the sun? Scientists had predicted there would be a group of comets not too far beyond Neptune, but no one had seen these objects. There were other people trying to find the same thing, so it was a bit of a race. We're glad we won it.

Q *Where did you start looking?*

A Most things in the solar system are in a plane, a basically flat disk where the planets and the sun are. So you start looking there. Then, you want to look opposite the sun. Also, you look at a time of the year when the Milky Way, our home galaxy, isn't in the part of the sky you're

These color-enhanced images of Jupiter (above), Saturn (right), and Neptune (below) were taken from a *Voyager* spacecraft.

searching. That's so the light of all those stars doesn't make it hard to see.

Q *Once you knew where to look, what did you do?*

A We took pictures. We started in 1987 and saw the first object in 1992, five years later. In the beginning we didn't have a computer at the telescope that was fast enough to analyze the pictures. So we'd make three pictures and then take them home to analyze. We'd take images, say a half-hour apart, of the same piece of sky. Then we'd look to see if any point of light had moved

These observatories are located on top of Mauna Kea, an inactive volcano in Hawaii.

between the three pictures. If it moves, we know it's near us in the solar system, and not a distant star. Since our first discovery in 1992, scientists have found about 60 objects in the Kuiper Belt. David and I have found about two thirds of those.

The Kuiper Belt lies beyond the part of the solar system where the planets revolve around the sun. Objects in the Kuiper Belt revolve far from Earth and the sun. Pluto's orbit is on a different plane from the other planets.

Q *Do you stay up all night?*

A Yes, we have to. Telescope time is valuable so you don't want to waste a single minute. We observe for a week or so, staying up for 5 or 6 nights in a row. It's hard work, switching from a daytime to a nighttime schedule. In Hawaii, we observe on top of Mauna Kea volcano at 14,000 feet. So we have to add an extra night at the beginning to get used to the altitude and thin air.

Kuiper Belt

Pluto

Neptune

Q *Five years is a long time to wait for a discovery. Didn't you get discouraged?*

A We told ourselves that after we'd covered a certain part of the sky without finding anything, we would stop. We were pretty near that limit. But the newer cameras could take bigger pictures of the sky. They helped us do in a month what at first had taken two years. We could see something and know right away where to look the next night.

Because I've been lucky, I've participated in discoveries. There's such a satisfaction you get when you solve a puzzle, when you find out something that nobody has known before. And it's really fun after a lot of hard work, when you've finally found what you wanted to find.

In Your Journal

Jane Luu describes working night after night for five years, observing and recording data for one part of the night sky. "It was so time-consuming, and we didn't know if anything was going to come from it." Fortunately, in the end, she was rewarded. How did Jane Luu's persistence, as well as her skill, energy, and step-by-step reasoning, lead to her success?

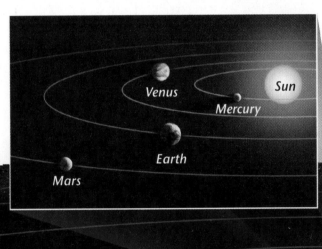

Venus

Mercury

Sun

Earth

Mars

Uranus

Jupiter

Saturn

CHAPTER 1

Earth, Moon, and Sun

 **WEB ACTIVITY** www.phschool.com

Where's the Moon?

What a view! Though you would have to be in orbit around the moon to see this kind of Earthrise, you don't have to travel at all to see the moonrise from Earth. All you have to do is look in the right direction at the right time and you will see the moon rise in front of you!

In this chapter, you will explore relationships among Earth, the moon, and the sun. In your project, you will observe the position of the moon in the sky every day. These observations will show you the changing positions of Earth and the moon with respect to each other and to the sun.

Your Goal To observe the shape of the moon and its position in the sky every day for one month.

To complete the project you will
◆ observe and record every day the compass direction in which you see the moon and its height above the horizon
◆ use your observations to explain the phases of the moon
◆ develop rules you can use to predict where and when you might see the moon each day throughout a month

Get Started Begin by preparing an observation log. You will want to record the date and time of each observation, the direction and height of the moon, a sketch of its shape, and notes about the cloud cover or other conditions. You can also keep track of the time of moonrise each day.

Check Your Progress You'll be working on this project as you study this chapter. To keep your project on track, look for Check Your Progress boxes at the following points.

Section 1 Review, page 21: Make a map to help you determine the direction of the moon.
Section 2 Review, page 34: Observe the moon every day.
Section 4 Review, page 44: Look for patterns in your observations.

Wrap Up At the end of the chapter (page 47), you will present your observations of the moon using words, drawings, and graphs.

This amazing Earthrise above the moon's horizon was seen by astronaut Michael Collins in the *Apollo 11* moon orbiter *Columbia*.

SECTION

4 Earth's Moon

Discover **Why Do Craters Look Different From Each Other?**
Sharpen Your Skills **Calculating**

SECTION
① Earth in Space

DISCOVER · ACTIVITY · · · ·

Why Does Earth Have Day and Night?

1. Place a lamp with a bare bulb in the middle of a table to represent the sun. Put a globe at the end of the table about 1 meter away to represent Earth.

2. Turn the lamp on and darken the room. Which parts of the globe have light shining on them? Which parts are in shadow?

3. Find your location on the globe. Take about 5 seconds to turn the globe once. Notice when it is lit—day—at your location and when it is dark—night.

Think It Over

Making Models How does one complete turn of the globe represent one day? In this model, how many seconds represent one day? How could you use the model to represent a year?

GUIDE FOR READING

◆ What causes day and night?

◆ What causes the cycle of seasons on Earth?

Reading Tip Before you read, preview the figures and captions in the section. List any terms that are not familiar to you. Then write their definitions as you read about them.

Ancient Egyptian farmers eagerly awaited the annual spring flood of the Nile River. For thousands of years, their planting was ruled by it. As soon as the Nile's floodwaters withdrew, the farmers had to be ready to plow and plant their fields along the banks of the river. Because of this, the Egyptians wanted to predict when the flood would occur. Around 3000 B.C., people noticed that the bright star Sirius first became visible in the early morning sky every year shortly before the flood began. The Egyptians used this knowledge to predict each year's flood.

Egyptian farmers ▶

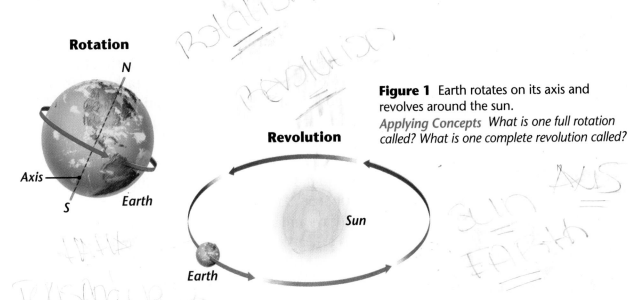

Rotation

N

Axis

S

Earth

Revolution

Earth

Sun

Figure 1 Earth rotates on its axis and revolves around the sun.
Applying Concepts *What is one full rotation called? What is one complete revolution called?*

Days and Years

The ancient Egyptians were among the first people to study the stars. The study of the moon, stars and other objects in space is called **astronomy.**

Ancient astronomers also studied the movements of the sun and the moon as they appeared to travel across the sky. It seemed to them as though Earth were standing still and the sun and moon were moving. Actually, the sun and moon seem to move across the sky each day mainly because Earth is rotating on its axis.

Rotation The imaginary line that passes through Earth's center and the North and South poles is called Earth's **axis.** The north end of the axis currently points toward a point in space near Polaris, the North Star. Earth's spinning on its axis is called its **rotation.** A point on the equator rotates at about 1,600 kilometers per hour. Even most commercial jet planes can't fly this fast!

Earth's rotation on its axis causes day and night. As Earth rotates eastward, the sun appears to move westward across the sky. It is day on the side of Earth facing the sun. As Earth continues to turn to the east, the sun appears to set in the west. Sunlight can't reach the side of Earth facing away from the sun, so it is night there. It takes Earth about 24 hours to rotate once on its axis. As you know, each 24-hour cycle of day and night is called a day.

Revolution In addition to rotating on its axis, Earth travels around the sun. The movement of one object around another object is called **revolution.** One complete revolution around the sun is called a year. Earth's path as it revolves around the sun is called its **orbit.** As it travels around the sun, Earth's orbit is not quite a circle. It is a slightly flattened circle, or oval shape.

✓ Checkpoint *Why do the sun and moon seem to move each day?*

Sharpen your *Skills*

Calculating

ACTIVITY

Earth moves at a speed of about 30 km/sec as it travels around the sun. What distance, in kilometers, does Earth travel in a minute? An hour? A day? A year?

Calendars The Egyptian astronomers counted the number of days between each first appearance of the star Sirius. In this way, they found that there were about 365 days in each year. By dividing the year into 365 days, the ancient Egyptians had created one of the first calendars.

People of many different cultures have struggled to come up with workable calendars. Earth's orbit around the sun takes slightly more than 365 days—actually about $365\frac{1}{4}$ days. Four years of about $365\frac{1}{4}$ days each can be approximated by taking 3 years of 365 days and a fourth year of 366 days. You know this fourth year as a "leap year." During a leap year, an extra day is

SCIENCE & History

Tracking the Cycle of the Year

For thousands of years, people have used observations of the sky to keep track of the time of year.

1500 B.C.
British Isles

Ancient peoples complete Stonehenge, a monument with giant stones that mark the directions in which the sun rises and sets on the longest day of the year.

| 1500 B.C. | 900 B.C. | 300 B.C. |

1300 B.C.
China

During the Shang dynasty, Chinese astronomers made detailed observations of the sun, planets, and other objects they saw in the night sky. Chinese astronomers calculated that the length of a year is 365.25 days.

300 B.C.
Egypt

Astronomers in Alexandria, Egypt, learned to use an instrument called an astrolabe. Astrolabes were used to find the positions of stars and planets.

added to February, giving it 29 days instead of its usual 28.

Dividing the year into smaller parts was difficult also. Early people used moon cycles as a sort of calendar. The time between one full moon and the next one is about $29\frac{1}{2}$ days. A year of 12 of these "moonths" only adds up to 354 days. The ancient Egyptians worked out a calendar that had 12 months of 30 days each, with an extra 5 days that were not part of any month. The Romans borrowed this calendar and made changes to it. With more changes, it eventually became the calendar we know: 11 months having 30 or 31 days each, plus one month (February) having 28 or 29 days.

In Your Journal

Research one of the accomplishments discussed in the time line. Write a dialogue in which two people from the culture that made the discovery or observation discuss its importance in their lives.

A.D. 1450
Wyoming

The Big Horn Medicine Wheel was built by Native Americans. Individual stones are aligned with the rising and setting sun and several bright stars. The rising of these specific stars may have indicated to people when it was time to move south for the winter.

A.D. 300	A.D. 900	A.D. 1500

A.D. 900
Mexico

The Mayas studied the movement of the sun, the moon, and the planet Venus. They had two different calendars, one with 365 days for everyday use and the other with 260 days for religious uses. These calendars combined to make a 52-year cycle. The Mayas were able to predict astronomical events 3,000 years into the future.

Figure 2 It is warm near the equator because sunlight hits Earth's surface directly and is less spread out. *Interpreting Diagrams* Why is it colder near the poles?

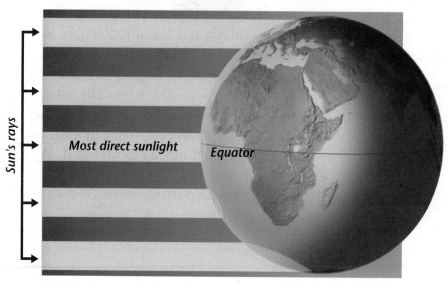

Sun's rays

Most direct sunlight   Equator

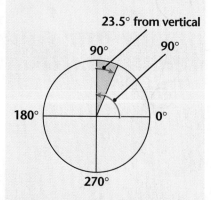

Angles

An angle is formed when two lines meet at a point. Angles are measured in degrees (symbol °). A full circle has 360 degrees.

23.5° from vertical

90°   90°

180°   0°

270°

Earth's axis is tilted at an angle of 23.5° from the vertical. When the sun is directly overhead at noon near the equator, its angle from the horizon is 90°. What fraction of a circle is this?

Seasons on Earth

Most places outside the tropics have four distinct seasons: winter, spring, summer, and autumn. But there are great differences in temperature from place to place. For instance, it is warmer near the equator than near the poles. Why is this so?

How Sunlight Hits Earth Figure 2 shows how sunlight hits Earth's surface. Notice that at the equator, sunlight hits Earth's surface directly. Closer to the poles, sunlight hits Earth's surface at an angle. Near the poles, energy from the sun is spread out over a greater area. That is why it is warmer near the equator than near the poles.

Earth's Tilted Axis If Earth's axis were straight up and down relative to the sun, as it appears in Figure 2, temperatures would remain fairly constant year-round. There would be no seasons. **Earth has seasons because its axis is tilted as it moves around the sun.**

Look at Earth's position in space in *Exploring the Seasons* on the next page. Notice that Earth's axis is tilted at an angle of 23.5° from the vertical. As Earth revolves around the sun, its axis is tilted away from the sun for part of the year and toward the sun for part of the year.

When the north end of Earth's axis is tilted toward the sun, the Northern Hemisphere has summer. At the same time, the south end of Earth's axis is tilted away from the sun. As a result, the Southern Hemisphere has winter.

Summer and winter are not affected by changes in Earth's distance from the sun. In fact, when the Northern Hemisphere is having summer, Earth is actually at its greatest distance from the sun.

EXPLORING *the Seasons*

The yearly cycle of the seasons is caused by the tilt of Earth's axis as it revolves around the sun.

March Equinox

June Solstice

September Equinox

Late December—Solstice
The south end of Earth's axis is tilted toward the sun. It is summer in the Southern Hemisphere and winter in the Northern Hemisphere.

December Solstice

Late June—Solstice
The north end of Earth's axis is tilted toward the sun. It is summer in the Northern Hemisphere and winter in the Southern Hemisphere.

Late March and Late September—Equinoxes
Neither end of Earth's axis is tilted toward the sun. Both hemispheres receive the same amount of energy.

June Solstice

N

Sun's rays

Equator

S

Noon sun vertical at 23.5° N

March Equinox

N

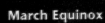

Sun's rays

Equator

S

Noon sun vertical at equator

December Solstice

N

Sun's rays

Equator

S

Noon sun vertical at 23.5° S

Earth in June In June, the north end of Earth's axis is tilted toward the sun. The noon sun is directly overhead at 23.5° north latitude. **Latitude** is a measurement of distance from the equator, expressed in degrees north or south. (The equator has latitude 0° and the North Pole has latitude 90° north.)

The hemisphere that is tilted toward the sun also has more hours of daylight than the hemisphere that is tilted away from the sun. The combination of direct rays and more hours of sunlight heats the surface more than at any other time of the year. It is summer in the Northern Hemisphere.

At the same time, for any place on Earth south of the equator, the sun's energy is spread over a large area. There are also fewer hours of daylight. The combination of indirect rays and fewer hours of sunlight heats Earth's surface less than at any other time of the year. It is winter in the Southern Hemisphere.

Earth in December Look again at *Exploring the Seasons.* Around December 21, the noon sun is overhead at 23.5° south latitude. People in the Southern Hemisphere receive the most direct sunlight, so it is summer there. At the same time, the sun's rays in the Northern Hemisphere are indirect and there are fewer hours of daylight. So it is winter in the Northern Hemisphere.

Both June and December On two days each year, the noon sun is overhead at either 23.5° south or 23.5° north. Each of these days is known as a **solstice** (SAHL stis). The day when the noon sun is overhead at 23.5° south is the winter solstice in the Northern Hemisphere. It is the summer solstice in the Southern Hemisphere. This solstice occurs around December 21 each year, and is the shortest day of the year in the Northern Hemisphere. At

Figure 3 Spring is the season between the vernal equinox and the summer solstice. The warming temperatures of spring make it the best time to plant flowers like these pansies.

the same time, it is close to the longest day of the year in the Southern Hemisphere.

Similarly, around June 21, the noon sun is overhead at 23.5° north. This is the summer solstice in the Northern Hemisphere and the winter solstice in the Southern Hemisphere.

Earth in March and September Halfway between the solstices, neither hemisphere is tilted toward or away from the sun. This situation only occurs on two days of the year. On these days, the noon sun is directly overhead at the equator.

Each of these days is known as an **equinox,** which means "equal night." During an equinox, the lengths of nighttime and daytime are about the same. The **vernal equinox,** or spring equinox, occurs around March 21, and marks the beginning of spring in the Northern Hemisphere. The **autumnal equinox** occurs around September 23. It marks the beginning of fall in the Northern Hemisphere.

![INTEGRATING LIFE SCIENCE] In much of the United States, seasonal changes affect living things. In spring and summer, the sun shines for more hours each day and is higher in the sky. The warmer days allow many plants to begin growing leaves and flowers. Because plants grow more, animals that feed on the plants, from tiny insects to large deer, get more food.

In the fall, the nights get longer, signaling the plants to stop growing and some plants to lose their leaves. With less food available, black bears and some other animals go into a dormant state in which they use very little energy. Others, like many songbirds and waterfowl, travel to warmer climates where food is still available.

Figure 4 This hungry bear has spent the long winter in a dormant state in a cave in Alaska.
Applying Concepts Why didn't this bear remain active all winter?

Section 1 Review

1. Explain the process that causes day and night.
2. What two factors cause the cycle of the seasons?
3. Compare rotation and revolution.
4. What do the words *solstice* and *equinox* mean? How are they related to the position of Earth's axis?
5. **Thinking Critically Relating Cause and Effect** Are changes in the distance between Earth and the sun important in causing the cycle of the seasons? Explain.

Check Your Progress

CHAPTER PROJECT 1

Begin recording your daily observations of the moon. Sketch a map of the site from which you will be making observations. Which way is north? East? South? West? Each night, observe and record the moon's direction. You should also estimate the moon's altitude, or height in degrees from the horizon. You can do this by making a fist and holding it at arm's length. One fist above the horizon is 10°, two fists are 20°, and so on.

REASONS FOR THE SEASONS

In this lab, you will use an Earth-sun model to make observations about factors that contribute to the seasons.

Problem

What effect does the tilt of Earth's axis have on the heat and light received by Earth as it revolves around the sun?

Materials (per pair of students)

books   flashlight   paper
pencil   protractor   toothpick
acetate sheet with thick grid lines drawn on it
plastic foam ball marked with poles and equator

Procedure

1. Make a pile of books about 15 cm high.
2. Tape the acetate sheet to the head of the flashlight. Place the flashlight on the pile of books.
3. Carefully push a pencil into the South Pole of the plastic foam ball, which represents Earth.
4. Use the protractor to measure a 23.5° tilt of the axis of your Earth away from your "flashlight sun," as shown in the first diagram. This represents winter.
5. Hold the pencil so that Earth is steady at this 23.5° angle and about 15 cm from the flashlight head. Turn the flashlight on. Dim the room lights.
6. The squares on the acetate should show up on your model Earth. Move the ball closer if necessary or dim the room lights more. Observe and record the shape of the squares at the equator and at the poles.

7. Carefully stick the toothpick straight into your model Earth about halfway between the equator and the North Pole. Observe and record the length of the shadow.
8. Without changing the tilt, turn the pencil to rotate the model Earth once on its axis. Observe and record how the shadow of the toothpick changes.
9. Tilt your model Earth 23.5° toward the flashlight, as shown in the second diagram. This is summer. Observe and record the shape of the squares at the equator and at the poles. Observe how the toothpick's shadow changes.
10. Rotate the model Earth and note the shadow pattern.

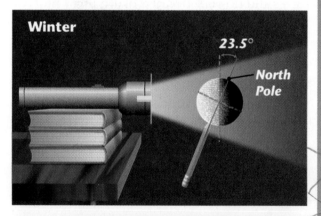

Winter

23.5°

North Pole

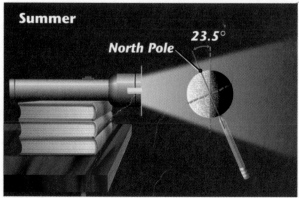

Summer

North Pole

23.5°

Analyze and Conclude

1. When it is winter in the Northern Hemisphere, which areas on Earth get the most concentrated amount of light? Which areas get the most concentrated light when it is summer in the Northern Hemisphere?

2. Compare your observations of how the light hits the area halfway between the equator and the North Pole during winter (Step 6) and during summer (Step 9).

3. If the squares projected on the ball from the acetate become larger, what can you conclude about the amount of heat distributed in each square?

4. According to your observations, which areas on Earth are consistently coolest? Which areas are consistently warmest? Why?

5. What time of year will the toothpick's shadow be longest? When will the shadow be shortest?

6. How are the amounts of heat and light received in a square related to the angle of the sun's rays?

7. **Think About It** How can you use your observations of an Earth-sun model to explain what causes the seasons?

More to Explore

You can measure how directly light from the sun hits Earth's surface by making a shadow stick. You need a stick or pole about 1 m long. With the help of your teacher, push the stick partway into the ground where it will not be disturbed. Make sure the stick stays vertical. At noon on the first day of every month, measure the length of the stick's shadow. The shorter the shadow, the more directly the sun's rays are hitting Earth. At what time of the year are the shadows longest? Shortest? How do your observations help explain the seasons?

SECTION 2 Phases, Eclipses, and Tides

DISCOVER

How Does the Moon Move?

1. Put a quarter flat on your desk to represent Earth. Use a penny flat on your desk to represent the moon.

2. One side of the moon always faces Earth. Move the moon through one revolution around Earth, keeping Lincoln's face always looking at Earth. How many times did the penny make one complete rotation?

Think It Over

Inferring From the point of view of someone on Earth, does the moon seem to rotate? Explain your answer.

GUIDE FOR READING

◆ What causes the phases of the moon?

◆ What causes solar and lunar eclipses?

◆ What causes the tides?

Reading Tip As you read, write a sentence to describe what causes each of the following: phases, solar eclipses, lunar eclipses, tides.

The moon is Earth's closest neighbor in space—much closer than any planet. In fact, the average distance from Earth to the moon is only about 30 times Earth's diameter. Even so, the moon is quite far away. On average, the moon is 384,400 kilometers from Earth. If there were a highway to the moon and you could travel at 100 kilometers per hour, it would take you more than five months to get there.

The moon moves in space just as Earth does. As the moon revolves around Earth and Earth revolves around the sun, the relative positions of the moon, Earth, and sun change. **The positions of the moon, Earth, and the sun cause the phases of the moon, eclipses, and tides.**

Motions of the Moon

The moon revolves around Earth and rotates on its own axis. It takes the moon about 27.3 days to revolve around Earth. Like Earth's orbit around the sun, the moon's orbit around Earth is a flattened circle or oval shape.

The moon rotates slowly on its own axis once every 27.3 days. Because the moon also revolves around Earth every 27.3 days, a "day" and a "year" on the moon are the same length. As you saw if you

◄ Crescent moon over Fire Island, New York

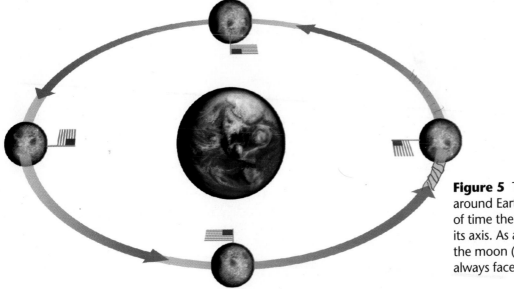

Figure 5 The moon revolves around Earth in the same amount of time the moon takes to rotate on its axis. As a result, the near side of the moon (shown with a flag) always faces Earth.

tried the Discover activity, the same side of the moon, the "near side," always faces Earth. The "far side" of the moon always faces away from Earth, so you never see it from Earth.

☑ *Checkpoint* *How many days does it take the moon to revolve once around Earth?*

Phases of the Moon

On a clear night when the moon is full, the bright moonlight can keep you awake. But the moon does not produce the light you see. Instead, it reflects light from the sun. Imagine taking a flashlight into a dark room. If you were to shine the flashlight on a chair, you would see the chair because the light from your flashlight would bounce, or reflect, off the chair. In the same way that the chair wouldn't shine by itself, the moon doesn't give off light by itself. You see the moon because sunlight reflects off it.

When you see the moon in the sky, sometimes it appears round. Other times you see only a thin sliver, or crescent. The different shapes of the moon you see from Earth are called **phases.** The moon goes through its whole set of phases each time it revolves around Earth, that is, about once a month.

What Causes Phases? Phases are caused by changes in the relative positions of the moon, Earth, and the sun. Because the sun lights the moon, half the moon is almost always in sunlight. However, since the moon revolves around Earth, you see the moon from different angles. The half of the moon that faces Earth is not always the half that is sunlit. **The phase of the moon you see depends on how much of the sunlit side of the moon faces Earth.** To understand the changing phases, refer to *Exploring Phases of the Moon* on the next page.

XPLORING Phases of the Moon

The diagram in the center shows a view of Earth and the moon phases from above. The sun is shining from the right. The outer ring of photos shows the different amounts of the sunlit side of the moon that an observer on Earth sees as the moon revolves around Earth.

First Quarter
You see half of the lighted side of the moon.

Waxing Crescent
You see more and more of the lighted side of the moon. This is called a waxing crescent moon.

Waxing Gibbous
The moon continues to wax. The moon is called gibbous.

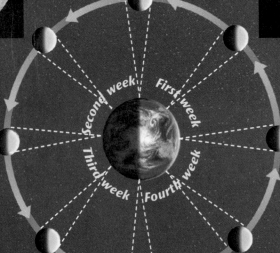

Second week / First week / Third week / Fourth week

New Moon
The sun lights the side of the moon facing away from Earth. The side of the moon that faces Earth is dark.

Full Moon
You see the whole lighted side of the moon.

Waning Gibbous
The fraction of the lighted side of the moon that you see gets smaller each day.

Third Quarter
You can see half of the moon's lighted side.

Waning Crescent
You see a crescent again.

The Cycle of the Phases During the new moon, the side of the moon facing Earth is not lit. As the moon revolves around Earth, you see more and more of the lighted side of the moon every day, until the side of the moon you see is fully lit. As the moon continues in its orbit, you see less and less of the lighted side of the moon. About 29.5 days after the last new moon, the cycle is complete, and you see a new moon again.

☑ *Checkpoint* *Since the moon does not produce light, how can you see it?*

Eclipses

What would you think if you were walking home from school on a sunny afternoon and the sun began to disappear? Would you be frightened? On rare occasions, the moon completely blocks the sun. The sky grows as dark as night even in the middle of a clear day. The air gets cool and the sky becomes an eerie color. If you don't know what is happening, you can become very frightened.

The moon doesn't usually go directly between Earth and the sun or directly behind Earth. As Figure 6 shows, the moon's orbit around Earth is slightly tilted with respect to Earth's orbit around the sun. As a result, in most months the moon revolves completely around Earth without the moon moving into Earth's shadow or the moon's shadow hitting Earth.

When the moon's shadow hits Earth or Earth's shadow hits the moon, an eclipse occurs. An **eclipse** (ih KLIPS) occurs when an object in space comes between the sun and a third object, and casts a shadow on that object. There are two types of eclipses: solar eclipses and lunar eclipses. (The words *solar* and *lunar* come from the Latin words for "sun" and "moon.")

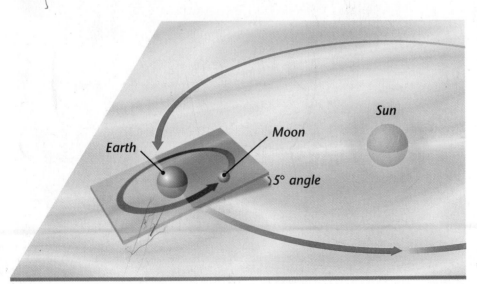

Earth

Moon

Sun

5° angle

Figure 6 The moon's orbit is tilted with respect to Earth's orbit. So the moon rarely goes directly between Earth and the sun.
Interpreting Diagrams How large is the angle between Earth's orbit and the moon's orbit?

Here is how you can draw a scale model of a solar eclipse. The moon's diameter is about one fourth Earth's diameter. The distance from Earth to the moon is about 30 times Earth's diameter. Make a scale drawing of the moon, Earth, and the distance between them. (*Hint:* Draw Earth 1 cm in diameter in one corner of the paper.) From the edges of the moon, draw and shade in a triangle just touching Earth to show the moon's umbra during a solar eclipse.

Solar Eclipses

During a new moon, the moon is almost exactly between Earth and the sun. But most months, as you have seen, the moon travels a little above or below the sun in the sky. A **solar eclipse** occurs when the moon passes between Earth and the sun, blocking the sunlight from reaching Earth. The moon's shadow then hits Earth, as shown in Figure 7. So a solar eclipse is really just a new moon in which the moon blocks your view of the sun.

Total Solar Eclipses The darkest part of the moon's shadow, the **umbra** (UM bruh), is cone-shaped. From any point in the umbra, light from the sun is completely blocked by the moon. The moon's umbra happens to be long enough so that the point of the cone can just reach a small part of Earth's surface. Only the people within the umbra experience a total solar eclipse. During a total solar eclipse, the sky is dark. You can see the stars and the solar corona, which is the faint outer atmosphere of the sun.

Partial Solar Eclipses In Figure 7, you can see that the moon casts another shadow that is less dark than the umbra. In this larger part of the shadow, called the **penumbra** (pih NUM bruh), part of the sun is visible from Earth. During a solar eclipse, people in the penumbra see only a partial eclipse. Since part of the sun remains visible, it is not safe to look directly at the sun during a partial solar eclipse (just as you wouldn't look directly at the sun at any other time).

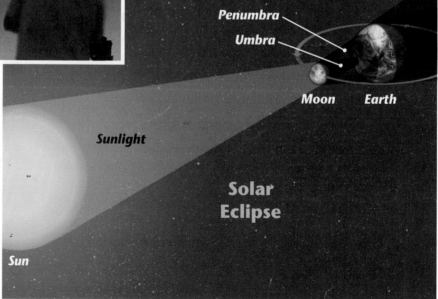

Penumbra

Umbra

Moon   Earth

Sunlight

Solar Eclipse

Sun

Figure 7 During a solar eclipse, right, the moon blocks light from the sun, preventing the light from reaching Earth's surface. The solar corona surrounding the dark disk of the moon, above, is visible during a solar eclipse.

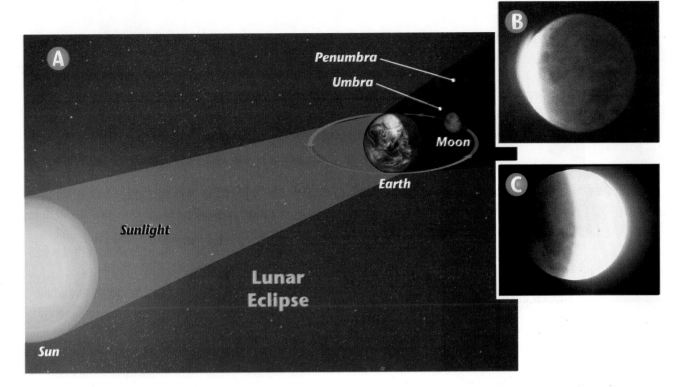

Figure 8 A. During a lunar eclipse, Earth blocks sunlight from reaching the moon's surface. B. This photo of the moon was taken during a total lunar eclipse. C. This photo was taken during a partial lunar eclipse. *Interpreting Diagrams What is the difference between Earth's umbra and penumbra?*

Lunar Eclipses

During most months, the moon goes near Earth's shadow but not quite into it. A **lunar eclipse** occurs at a full moon when Earth is directly between the moon and the sun. You can see a lunar eclipse in Figure 8. During a lunar eclipse, Earth blocks sunlight from reaching the moon. The moon is then in Earth's shadow and looks dark from Earth. Because the moon is closest to Earth's shadow during the full moon, lunar eclipses occur only at full moon.

Total Lunar Eclipses Like the moon's shadow, Earth's shadow has an umbra and a penumbra. When the moon is in Earth's umbra, you see a total lunar eclipse. You can see Earth's shadow on the moon before and after the total part of a lunar eclipse.

Unlike a solar eclipse, a lunar eclipse can be seen anywhere on Earth that the moon is visible. So you are more likely to see a total lunar eclipse than a total solar eclipse.

Partial Lunar Eclipses For most lunar eclipses, Earth, the moon, and the sun are not quite in line, and a partial lunar eclipse results. A partial lunar eclipse occurs when the moon passes partly into the umbra of Earth's shadow. The edge of the umbra appears blurry, and you can watch it pass across the moon for two or three hours.

✓ *Checkpoint* *Why do lunar eclipses occur only at full moon?*

A "Moonth" of Phases

In this lab, you will use a model of the Earth-moon-sun system to explore how the phases of the moon occur.

Problem

What causes the phases of the moon?

Materials

floor lamp with 150-watt bulb
pencils
plastic foam balls

Procedure

1. Place a lamp in the center of the room. Remove the lampshade.
2. Close the doors and shades to darken the room, and switch on the lamp.
3. Carefully stick the point of a pencil into the plastic foam ball so that the pencil can be used as a "handle."
4. Draw 8 circles on a sheet of paper. Number them 1–8.
5. Have your partner hold the plastic foam ball at arm's length in front and slightly above his or her head so that the ball is between him or her and the lamp. **CAUTION:** *Do not look directly at the bulb.*
6. The ball should be about 1 to 1.5 m away from the lamp. Adjust the distance between the ball and the lamp so that the light shines brightly on the ball.

7. Stand directly behind your partner and observe what part of the ball facing you is lit by the lamp. If light is visible on the ball, draw the shape of the lighted part of the ball in the first circle.
8. Have your partner turn 45° to the left while keeping the ball in front and at arm's length.
9. Repeat Step 7. Be sure you are standing directly behind your partner.
10. Repeat Steps 8 and 9 six more times until your partner is facing the lamp again. See the photograph for the 8 positions.
11. Change places and repeat Steps 4–10.

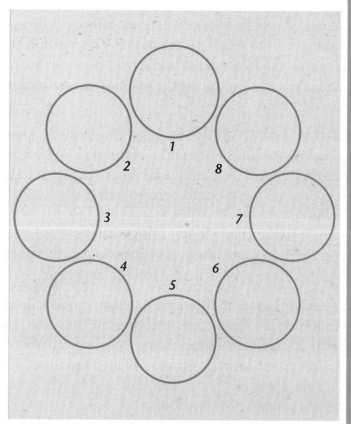

Analyze and Conclude

1. In your model, what represents Earth? The sun? The moon?
2. Refer back to your 8 circles. How much of the lighted part of the ball did you see when facing the lamp?
3. Label your drawings with the names of the phases of the moon. Which drawing represents a full moon? A new moon? Which represents a waxing crescent? A waning crescent?
4. How much of the lighted part of the ball did you see after each turn?
5. Whether you could see it or not, how much of the ball's surface was always lit by the lamp? Was the darkness of the new moon caused by an eclipse? Explain your answer.
6. **Think It Over** How did making a model help you understand the phases of the moon? What are some disadvantages of using models? What is another way to make a model to represent the moon's phases?

More to Explore

Design a model to show a lunar eclipse and a solar eclipse. What objects would you use for Earth, the sun, and the moon? Use the model to demonstrate why there isn't an eclipse every full moon and new moon.

45°

Figure 9 The Hopewell Rocks in New Brunswick, Canada, are partly covered at high tide. At low tide, people can walk along the beach between the rocks. *Predicting What would happen if these people stayed on the beach too long?*

Tides

Have you ever built a sand castle at an ocean beach? Was it washed away by the rising water? People who spend time near the ocean see the effects of **tides,** the rise and fall of water, every 12.5 hours or so. The water rises for about six hours, then falls for about six hours, in a regular cycle.

What Causes Tides? The force of **gravity** pulls the moon and Earth (including the water on Earth's surface) toward each other. The force of gravity between two objects depends on the masses of the objects and the distance between them. **Tides occur mainly because of differences in how much the moon pulls on different parts of Earth.**

As Earth rotates, the moon's gravity pulls water toward the point on Earth's surface closest to the moon. If that were the only cause, there would be only one high tide at a time, at the point on Earth closest to the moon. Actually, there is a second high tide on the opposite side of Earth, so the explanation must be more complex. The two tides occur because of the difference in the force of gravity from one place to another.

High Tides Look at Figure 10. The force of the moon's gravity at point A, which is closer to the moon, is stronger than the force of the moon's gravity on Earth as a whole. The water near point A is pulled toward the moon more strongly than is Earth as a whole. The water flows toward point A, and a high tide forms.

The force of the moon's gravity at point B, which is farther from the moon, is weaker than the force of the moon's gravity on Earth as a whole. Earth as a whole is pulled toward the moon more strongly than the water at point B, so the water is "left behind." Water flows toward point B, and a high tide occurs there too.

☑ *Checkpoint Why are there high tides on opposite sides of Earth at the same time?*

High and Low Tides

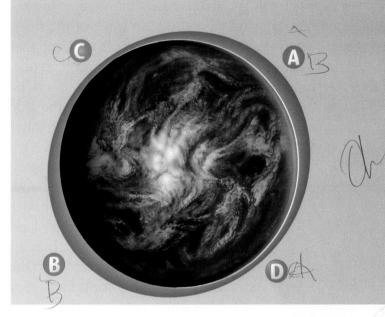

Point A
Closest to the moon, the moon pulls on water at Earth's surface more strongly than on Earth as a whole. Water flows toward Point A, creating a high tide.

Point B
Farthest away from the moon, the moon pulls less strongly on the water at Earth's surface than on Earth as a whole. Earth is pulled away from this point, leaving the water behind. The water that is left behind creates another high tide.

Points C and D
Low tides occur between the two high tides.

Figure 10 Tides occur mainly because of differences in the force of gravity between the moon and different parts of Earth.

The Tide Cycle Between points A and B, water flows away from points C and D, causing low tides to occur. Figure 10 shows that at any one time there are two places with high tides and two places with low tides on Earth. As Earth rotates, one high tide stays on the side of Earth facing the moon. The second high tide stays on the opposite side of Earth. Every location on Earth sweeps through those two high tides and two low tides in a 25-hour cycle.

Spring and Neap Tides The sun's gravity also pulls on Earth's waters. Once a month, at new moon, the sun, Earth, and moon are nearly in a line. The gravity of the sun and the moon pull in the same direction. The combined forces produce a tide with the greatest difference between low and high tide, called a **spring tide.**

What do you think happens at full moon? The moon and the sun are on opposite sides of Earth. However, since there are tides on both sides of Earth, a spring tide is also produced. It doesn't matter in which order the sun, Earth, and moon line up. So spring tides occur twice a month, at the new moon and at the full moon.

Also twice a month, during the moon's first quarter and last quarter phases, the line between Earth and the sun is at right angles to the line between Earth and the moon. The sun's pull is at right angles to the moon's. This arrangement produces a tide with the least difference between low and high tide, called a **neap tide.**

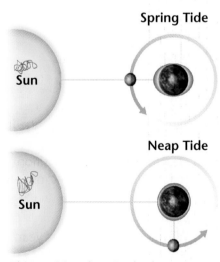

Figure 11 When Earth, the sun, and the moon are in a straight line (top), a spring tide occurs. When the moon is at a right angle to the sun (bottom), a neap tide occurs.

Figure 12 Purple sea stars feed on barnacles at low tide in an intertidal zone in Olympic National Park in Washington State. Both animals have adaptations for keeping moist and holding on that allow them to survive the ever-changing conditions of an intertidal zone.

Local Tide Effects Not every place on Earth has two regular tides every day. The shapes of bays, inlets, and the ocean floor can affect the flow of water, so that the height and timing of the tides can vary even in places that are close to each other. Because low tides can expose rocks and make waters too shallow to navigate, it is very important for sailors to keep track of the tides. Even today, you sometimes read in the newspaper that a ship that had run aground at low tide was floated off on the next high tide.

Sometimes, the effects of ocean tides extend far up rivers. Water at the river's mouth flows upstream as the tide comes in. As the tide changes and goes out, the water flows downstream back into the ocean.

INTEGRATING LIFE SCIENCE On many seashores, there is a strip of land, called an intertidal zone, that is under water at high tide but becomes dry land at low tide. Animals that live in intertidal zones must be adapted to the constantly changing conditions. Sea stars, for example, have powerful suction structures on the undersides of their arms. These allow sea stars to firmly stick to surfaces so they don't float away when tides rush in or out. Barnacles have hard plates on their shells that can clamp shut. This way, water stays inside their shells, keeping their soft bodies moist even when the tide is out.

Section 2 Review

1. Why does the moon change its phases as the month progresses?
2. Describe the relative positions of Earth, the sun, and the moon during a solar eclipse and during a lunar eclipse.
3. Explain why there are two high tides and two low tides each day.
4. Why are a "day" and a "year" on the moon the same length?
5. **Thinking Critically** **Interpreting Diagrams** Make a diagram to show what phase the moon is in during a lunar eclipse.

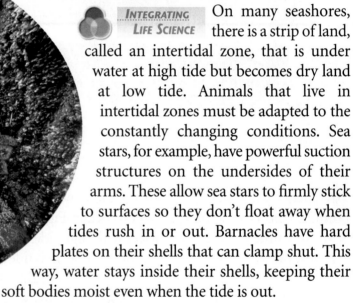

Check Your Progress

CHAPTER PROJECT 1

Bring your log sheet to class so you can share your observations with classmates. Check the newspaper every day to find the times of moonrise and moonset and record this information. If you can, look for the moon at moonrise or moonset, even during daylight hours. Use your map to keep track of the direction in which you can see the moon.

SECTION 3 Rockets and Satellites

DISCOVER

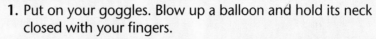

How Do Rockets Work?

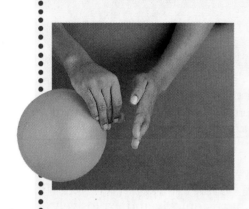

1. Put on your goggles. Blow up a balloon and hold its neck closed with your fingers.

2. Point the balloon toward an area where there are no people. Put your free hand behind the neck of the balloon, so the air will push against your hand. Let go of the balloon.

3. Repeat Steps 1 and 2 without your free hand behind the balloon.

Think It Over

Observing In which direction does the air rush out? In which direction does the balloon go? Does the balloon need to push against something in order to move? Explain your answer.

Curiosity about Earth's "neighborhood" in space has led to moon missions, space shuttle missions, space stations, and Mars missions. But without rockets, none of these accomplishments would have been possible.

How Rockets Work

A rocket works in much the way that a balloon is propelled through the air by releasing gas. **A rocket moves forward when gases expelled from the rear of the rocket push it in the opposite direction.** It's a basic law of physics that for every force, or action, there is an equal and opposite force, or reaction. For example, the force of the air going out the back of a balloon is an action force. An equal force, the reaction, pushes the balloon forward.

In a rocket, fuel is burned to make a hot gas. This hot gas is forced out of narrow nozzles in the back of the rocket, propelling the rocket forward.

GUIDE FOR READING

◆ How do rockets travel in space?

◆ What are satellites and space stations used for?

Reading Tip Before you read, rewrite the headings in the section as *how, why,* or *what* questions. As you read, look for answers to those questions.

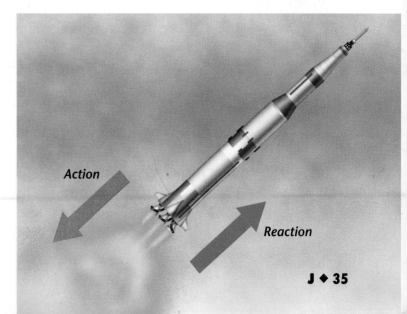

Figure 13 Hot gas is propelled out of the back of a rocket engine. The force of the gas in one direction (action) produces an opposing force (reaction) that propels the rocket forward.

Action

Reaction

4b Lunar vehicle proceeds to lunar orbit.

3b Third stage ignites.

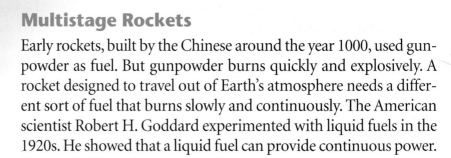

3a Second stage separates and falls to Earth.

4a Third stage is discarded.

2b Second stage ignites and continues with third stage.

2a First stage separates and falls to Earth.

Figure 14 Multistage rockets have three stages, or sections. Each of the first two stages burns all its fuel and then drops off. The next stage then takes over. Only part of the third stage reaches the rocket's destination.

Multistage Rockets

Early rockets, built by the Chinese around the year 1000, used gunpowder as fuel. But gunpowder burns quickly and explosively. A rocket designed to travel out of Earth's atmosphere needs a different sort of fuel that burns slowly and continuously. The American scientist Robert H. Goddard experimented with liquid fuels in the 1920s. He showed that a liquid fuel can provide continuous power. Some solid fuels also burn slowly and continuously.

Another problem remained, however. A rocket can carry only so much fuel. Once the fuel is used up, the rocket falls back to Earth. In 1903, a Russian named Konstantin Tsiolkovsky came up with the idea of multistage rockets. As each stage, or section, of a rocket uses up its fuel, the empty fuel container drops off. Then the next stage ignites and continues up toward the rocket's destination.

The development of powerful multistage rockets in the 1950s and 1960s made it possible to send rockets to the moon and farther into space. Figure 14 shows a rocket similar to the Saturn V that carried the astronauts to the moon. You will learn more about the moon landings in Section 4.

Artificial Satellites

The world was astounded on October 4, 1957, when the Soviet Union launched the first artificial satellite into orbit around Earth. A **satellite** is any natural or artificial object that revolves around an object in space, just as the moon revolves around Earth. This satellite, *Sputnik 1*, revolved around Earth every 96 minutes. Three months later, the United States launched *Explorer 1* into orbit. On April 12, 1961, Yuri Gagarin, a Soviet cosmonaut, orbited Earth, becoming the first person in space.

Third stage

Second stage

First stage

1 Heavy first stage provides thrust for launch.

Since 1957, thousands of artificial satellites, including space stations, have been launched into orbit. **Satellites and space stations are used for communications, navigation, collecting weather data, and research.**

Satellites Artificial satellites are used to relay telephone calls, to measure Earth's atmosphere, and to photograph weather systems, crops, troops, and ships. In addition, two dozen Global Positioning Satellites give off signals that can be picked up by small receivers on Earth. The receiver can then tell you where you are on Earth's surface.

Some satellites are in **geosynchronous orbits,** which means they revolve around Earth at the same rate that Earth rotates. Geosynchronous satellites above the equator seem to hover over a given point on Earth. Geosynchronous satellites are used to relay television signals and to map weather patterns.

Space Stations A space station is a large satellite in which people can live for long periods. The first space station, the Soviet Union's *Salyut,* was launched in 1971. In 1973, the United States launched *Skylab,* which carried a series of telescopes and scientific experiments. The former Soviet Union, of which Russia was part, launched the *Mir* space station in 1986. Astronauts from many countries, including Americans, visited *Mir.* Sixteen countries, including the United States and Russia, are cooperating on the International Space Station, which is now being built in orbit and will eventually provide living quarters and labs for up to seven astronauts.

☑ *Checkpoint* *What is a geosynchronous orbit?*

Be a Rocket Scientist

You can build a rocket.

1. Use a plastic or paper cup as the rocket body. Cut out a paper nose cone and tape it to the closed end of the cup.

2. Obtain an empty film canister with a lid that snaps on inside the canister. Go outside to do Steps 3–5.

3. Fill the canister about one-quarter full with water.

4. Put on your goggles. Now add half of a fizzing antacid tablet to the film canister and quickly snap on the lid.

5. Place the canister on the ground with the lid down. Place your rocket over the canister and stand back.

Observing What action happened inside the film canister? What was the reaction of the rocket?

Figure 15 The International Space Station is a cooperative project involving 16 countries, including the United States, Russia, Japan, and Canada. This is an artist's conception of the station in orbit.

Figure 16 The Space Shuttle *Discovery* is launched into space by its own rockets as well as by rockets attached to it. *Inferring What is one advantage of a reusable space vehicle?*

Space Shuttles

The Saturn V rockets that carried astronauts to the moon in the 1960s and 1970s were very expensive. In addition, they could not be reused because each stage burned up as it fell back through Earth's atmosphere. In the late 1970s, the National Aeronautics and Space Administration (NASA) developed the reusable space shuttles. They are called shuttles because they can go back and forth, or shuttle, between Earth and space. Since the first shuttle was launched in 1981, space shuttles have been the main way that the United States launches astronauts and equipment into space.

NASA is studying several ideas for building better and less expensive ways of launching people and cargo into space. The ideal vehicle would be an aerospace plane that could take off from a runway, travel into space, and land again on a runway.

Section 3 Review

Science at Home

1. How does a rocket work?
2. Describe three uses of satellites and space stations.
3. Which stage of a multistage rocket reaches the final destination?
4. **Thinking Critically Comparing and Contrasting** What is one way that Saturn V rockets and space shuttles are different?

Interview someone who remembers the space programs of the 1950s and 1960s. Prepare your questions in advance, such as: How did you feel when you heard that *Sputnik* was in orbit? How did you feel when the first Americans went into space? Did you watch any of the space flights on television? You may want to record your interview, then write it out in a question-and-answer format.

SECTION
4 Earth's Moon

DISCOVER •• ACTIVITY

Why Do Craters Look Different From Each Other?

The moon's surface has pits in it, called craters.

1. Put on your goggles. Fill a large plastic basin with 2 cm of sand.

2. Drop marbles of different masses from about 20 cm high. Take the marbles out and view the craters they left.

3. Predict what will happen if you drop marbles from a higher point. Smooth out the sand. Now drop marbles of different masses from about 50 cm high.

4. Take the marbles out and view the craters they left.

Think It Over

Developing Hypotheses In which step do you think the marbles were moving faster when they hit the sand? If objects hitting the moon caused craters, how did the speeds of the objects affect the sizes of the craters? How did the masses of the objects affect the sizes of the craters?

Would you want to take a vacation on the moon? Before you answer, think about these facts. There is no air or liquid water on the moon. Temperatures on the moon's surface range from 100°C, the boiling point of water, to –170°C, well below freezing.

To stay at a comfortable temperature and carry an air supply, the astronauts who landed on the moon had to wear bulky spacesuits. Each spacesuit had a mass of 90 kilograms, about as much as the astronaut himself! Because the moon's gravity is only about one-sixth as strong as Earth's, however, the astronauts were able to leap about like basketball stars despite their heavy spacesuits. What do you think now? Do you still want to go?

GUIDE FOR READING

◆ What features of the moon can be seen with a telescope?

◆ How did the Apollo landings help scientists learn about the moon?

Reading Tip As you read, write down ways in which the moon's surface is similar to Earth's surface.

Figure 17 Astronaut John W. Young jumps up from the moon's surface as he salutes the flag on April 21, 1972. The machine on the left is the *Apollo 16* lunar lander.

Figure 18 The diameter of the moon is a little less than the distance across the United States.

The Structure and Origin of the Moon

The moon is 3,476 kilometers in diameter, a little less than the distance across the United States. This diameter is only one fourth Earth's diameter. However, the moon contains only one-eightieth as much mass as Earth. Though Earth has a very dense core, the outer layers are less dense. The moon's average density is about the same as the density of Earth's outer layers.

People have long wondered how the moon formed. Scientists have suggested many possible hypotheses. For example, did Earth at one time spin so fast that the material the moon is made of was thrown off? Was the moon formed elsewhere in the solar system and captured by Earth's gravitational pull as it came near? Was the moon formed near Earth at the same time that Earth formed? Scientists have found reasons to reject all of these ideas.

The theory of the moon's origin that best fits the evidence is called the collision theory. It is illustrated in Figure 19. About 4.5 billion years ago, when Earth was very young, an object at least as large as Mars collided with Earth. Material from the object and Earth's outer layers was thrown into orbit around Earth. Eventually, this material combined to form the moon.

Looking at the Moon From Earth

For thousands of years, people could see shapes on the surface of the moon, but didn't know what caused them. The ancient Greeks thought that the moon was perfectly smooth. It was not until about 400 years ago that scientists could study the moon more closely.

Figure 19 This computer simulation shows the collision theory of the moon's origin. In this theory, a large object struck Earth. The resulting debris formed the moon.

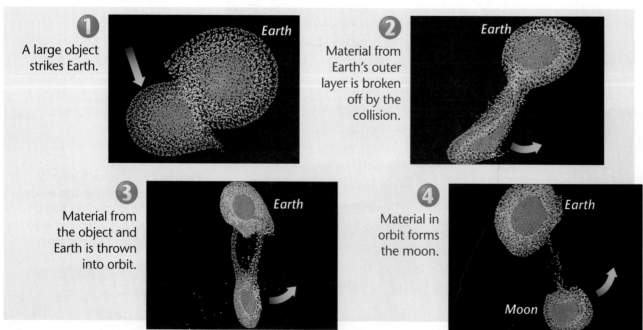

① A large object strikes Earth.

② Material from Earth's outer layer is broken off by the collision.

③ Material from the object and Earth is thrown into orbit.

④ Material in orbit forms the moon.

Plato

Sea of Rains

Archimedes

Sea of Serenity

Copernicus

Sea of Tranquillity

Figure 20 Astronomers have given names to many of the moon's craters and maria. Copernicus is one of the largest craters.

In 1609, the Italian astronomer Galileo Galilei heard about a device that made distant objects appear closer. Galileo soon made his own **telescope** by putting two lenses in a wooden tube. The lenses focused the light coming through the tube, making distant objects seem closer. When Galileo pointed his telescope at the moon, he was able to see much more detail than anyone had ever seen before. **Features on the moon's surface include craters, highlands, and maria.**

Galileo saw that much of the moon's surface is covered with round pits called **craters.** Some craters are hundreds of kilometers across. For 300 years, scientists thought that the craters on the moon had been made by volcanoes. But about 50 years ago, scientists concluded that the craters on the moon were caused by the impacts of meteoroids, rocks from space.

Galileo inferred that some of the other features he saw were highlands, or mountains. The peaks of the highlands and the rims of the craters cast dark shadows, which Galileo could see.

The moon's surface also has dark, flat areas, which Galileo called **maria** (MAH ree uh), the Latin word for "seas." Each one is a "mare" (MAH ray). Galileo thought that the maria might be oceans. Scientists now know that there are no oceans on the moon. The maria are low, dry areas that were flooded with molten material billions of years ago. Since you always see the same maria from Earth, you can tell that the moon always shows the same face to Earth.

☑ *Checkpoint* **What are maria?**

Visual Arts
CONNECTION

When Galileo observed the moon, he drew pictures like the one below. Galileo had been trained as an artist, so he interpreted his observations as an artist would. Light and shadow are used in art to create the appearance of three-dimensional forms.

Galileo saw the areas of light and shadow on the moon and concluded that the surface of the moon was not smooth.

In Your Journal

Under a bright light, set up an arrangement of objects. Sketch the outline of the objects. Then observe where the shadows fall. Shade in those areas. Notice how adding shading makes your drawing look more real.

Missions to the Moon

"I believe that this nation should commit itself to achieving the goal, before this decade is out, of landing a man on the moon and returning him safely to Earth." With these words from a May 1961 speech, President John F. Kennedy launched an enormous program of space exploration and scientific research.

Exploring the Moon Between 1964 and 1972, the United States and the Soviet Union sent dozens of rockets to explore the moon. Until spacecraft went to the moon, no one knew what its surface was like. Would spacecraft landing on the moon sink deep into thick dust and be lost? When *Surveyor* spacecraft landed on the moon, they didn't sink in, thus showing that the surface was solid. Lunar orbiters then photographed the moon's surface, so scientists could find a flat, safe spot for a rocket to land.

The Moon Landings In July 1969 three astronauts circled the moon in *Apollo 11*. Once in orbit around the moon, Neil Armstrong and Buzz Aldrin got into a tiny Lunar Module called *Eagle*, leaving Michael Collins in orbit in the Command Module. On July 20, 1969, the *Eagle* descended toward a flat area on the moon's surface called the Sea of Tranquillity. Armstrong and Aldrin were running out of fuel, so they had to find a safe landing spot fast. Billions of people held their breaths as they waited to learn if the astronauts had landed safely on the moon. Finally, a red light flashed on the control panel. "Contact light! Houston, Tranquillity Base here. The *Eagle* has landed," Armstrong radioed to Earth.

After the landing, Armstrong and Aldrin left the *Eagle* to explore the moon. When Armstrong first set foot on the moon, he said, "That's one small step for man, one giant leap for mankind." Armstrong meant to say "That's one small step for *a* man," meaning himself, but in his excitement he never said the "a."

Figure 21 On July 20, 1969, *Apollo 11* astronaut Neil Armstrong became the first person to walk on the moon. He took this photograph of Buzz Aldrin, the second person to walk on the moon. *Inferring Why was it important for the lunar module to land on a flat spot?*

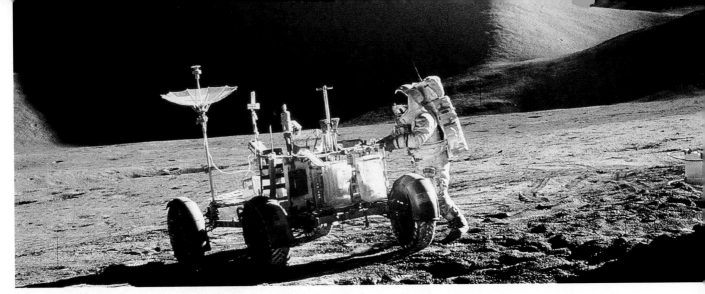

Figure 22 Astronauts on later missions had a lunar buggy to help them explore the moon's surface.

On the Surface of the Moon Everything the *Apollo 11* astronauts found was new and exciting. Even looking at their footprints taught the astronauts lessons about the moon's soil. The astronauts bounded around the surface, picking up samples of rocks to bring back to Earth for scientists to study.

In later missions, the astronauts were able to stay on the moon for days instead of hours. They even had a lunar buggy to ride around in. The astronauts were also able to land near the highlands, which were more interesting to study than the flat mare where *Apollo 11* landed.

Moon Rocks and Moonquakes The astronauts brought back to Earth 382 kilograms of moon rocks, about half the mass of a small car. **Much of what scientists have learned about the moon came from detailed study of the moon rocks gathered by astronauts.** Almost all of the rocks were formed from the cooling of molten material, so the moon's surface must once have been very hot. Some of the rocks showed that they had been broken apart by impacts and then reformed. So scientists concluded that meteoroids had bombarded the moon's surface.

The astronauts brought measuring instruments to the moon to record some of the meteoroid impacts. One type of device, known as a seismometer, is used to detect earthquakes on Earth. The seismometers on the moon detected extremely weak moonquakes, the result of changes deep under the moon's surface.

Until the *Apollo* astronauts landed, scientists knew very little about the moon's interior. Another kind of instrument the astronauts left behind measured the amount of heat flowing out from the moon's interior, in order to study what the inside of the moon is like. This instrument showed that the moon has cooled almost completely since it was formed.

✓ *Checkpoint* *What did scientists discover about the interior of the moon as a result of the moon landings?*

Sharpen your Skills

Calculating ACTIVITY

If you went to the moon for a vacation, your weight would only be about one sixth of your weight on Earth. To find your weight on the moon, divide your weight by 6.

If you had to wear a spacesuit that weighed as much as you do, what would be your total weight on the moon?

Figure 23 The far side of the moon is much rougher than the side that faces Earth.
Observing *What are the round features in this photograph called?*

Photographs of the Moon The *Apollo* astronauts circled the moon by rocket and photographed all parts of its surface. The pictures show that the far side of the moon is rougher than the near side and has very few maria.

The American *Clementine* spacecraft went to the moon in 1994. It took photographs of the moon through different filters chosen to show what types of minerals are on the moon. The name *Clementine* was chosen because it is the name of the prospector's daughter in the old song "My Darlin' Clementine."

In 1998, the American *Lunar Prospector* spacecraft went to the moon. *Lunar Prospector* mapped the entire moon from an altitude of only 100 kilometers. *Lunar Prospector* found evidence that there is ice frozen into the lunar soil near the moon's poles.

Section 4 Review

1. Name the three kinds of features that Galileo saw on the moon's surface.
2. What did the *Apollo* astronauts do on the moon?
3. How did the craters form on the moon?
4. **Thinking Critically** **Inferring** Why did scientists once think there were volcanoes on the moon? What evidence from the *Apollo* landings makes this unlikely?

Check Your Progress

CHAPTER PROJECT

1

Compare your observations of the moon early in the day with observations later that day. How does the moon appear to move in the sky during the course of the day? What happens to the appearance of the moon between earlier and later observations? Is there a pattern for each day? (*Hint:* See whether the same pattern holds true for observations later in the month.)

SECTION 1 Earth in Space

Key Ideas

- Astronomy is the study of the moon, stars, and other objects in space.
- Earth's rotation on its axis causes day and night.
- One complete revolution of Earth around the sun is called a year.
- Earth has seasons because its axis is tilted as it revolves around the sun.

Key Terms

astronomy	latitude
axis	solstice
rotation	equinox
revolution	vernal equinox
orbit	autumnal equinox

 ## SECTION 2 Phases, Eclipses, and Tides

Key Ideas

- The moon revolves around Earth and rotates on its own axis.
- The phase of the moon you see depends on how much of the sunlit side of the moon faces Earth.
- A solar eclipse occurs when the moon passes between Earth and the sun, blocking the sunlight from reaching Earth.
- A lunar eclipse occurs when Earth is directly between the moon and the sun, blocking the sunlight from reaching the moon.
- Tides occur mainly because of differences in how much the moon pulls on different parts of Earth.

Key Terms

phase	lunar eclipse
eclipse	tide
solar eclipse	gravity
umbra	spring tide
penumbra	neap tide

 ## SECTION 3 Rockets and Satellites

INTEGRATING TECHNOLOGY

Key Ideas

- A rocket moves in one direction when gases are expelled from it in the opposite direction.
- Satellites and space stations are used for communications, navigation, collecting weather data, and research.

Key Terms

satellite	geosynchronous orbit

SECTION 4 Earth's Moon

Key Ideas

- Features on the moon's surface include craters, highlands, and maria.
- Much of what scientists have learned about the moon came from detailed study of the moon rocks.

Key Terms

telescope	crater	maria

Organizing Information

Concept Map Copy the concept map about how Earth moves in space onto a sheet of paper. Then complete it and add a title. (For more on concept maps, see the Skills Handbook.)

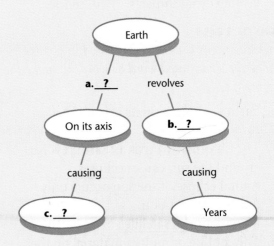

Reviewing Content

 For more review of key concepts, see the Interactive Student Tutorial CD-ROM.

Multiple Choice

Choose the letter of the answer that best completes each statement.

1. The movement of Earth around the sun once a year is Earth's
   a. orbit.
   b. rotation.
   c. revolution.
   d. axis.

2. The darkest part of a shadow is the
   a. umbra.
   b. penumbra.
   c. eclipse.
   d. phase.

3. When Earth's shadow falls on the moon, the shadow causes a
   a. new moon.
   b. solar eclipse.
   c. full moon.
   d. lunar eclipse.

4. A satellite in geosynchronous orbit revolves around Earth once each
   a. hour.
   b. week.
   c. month.
   d. day.

5. The craters on the moon were caused by
   a. highlands.   b. volcanoes.
   c. meteoroid impacts.   d. maria.

True or False

If the statement is true, write true. If it is false, change the underlined word or words to make the statement true.

6. Earth's spinning on its axis is called <u>revolution</u>.

7. The tilt of Earth's axis as Earth revolves around the sun causes <u>eclipses</u>.

8. A total eclipse of the <u>sun</u> occurs only during a new moon.

9. Many <u>artificial satellites</u> orbit Earth.

10. The cooling of molten material on the moon formed the <u>craters</u>.

Checking Concepts

11. Describe the shape of Earth's orbit.

12. Mars's axis is tilted at about the same angle as Earth's axis. Do you think Mars has seasons? Explain your answer.

13. How does the time it takes the moon to rotate on its axis compare with the time it takes the moon to revolve around Earth?

14. Why isn't there a lunar eclipse every month?

15. Why do more people see a total lunar eclipse than a total solar eclipse?

16. Why is there a high tide on the side of Earth closest to the moon? On the side of Earth furthest from the moon?

17. What basic law of physics explains how a rocket moves forward?

18. Describe the events that formed the moon, according to the collision theory.

19. What did scientists learn by studying the rocks astronauts brought back from the moon?

20. **Writing to Learn** Imagine that trips to the moon are resuming. You are an astronaut going to the moon. Write a paragraph describing what you see as you arrive. What does the sky look like? What could the rocks you find help scientists learn?

Thinking Critically

21. **Relating Cause and Effect** How do the changing positions of the moon, Earth, and sun cause spring tides or neap tides on Earth?

22. **Applying Concepts** At what time does the full moon rise? Is it visible in the eastern sky or the western sky?

23. **Posing Questions** Suppose you were assigned to design a spacesuit for astronauts to wear on the moon. What questions about the moon would you need to have answered in order to design the spacesuit?

Applying Skills

Use the illustration below to answer Questions 24–26. (*Hint:* The tilt of the Earth's axis is 23.5°.)

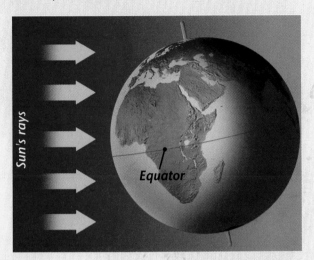

Equator

24. **Interpreting Diagrams** On which hemisphere are the sun's rays falling most directly?
25. **Inferring** In the Northern Hemisphere, is it the summer solstice, winter solstice, or one of the equinoxes? How do you know?

26. **Predicting** Six months after this illustration, Earth will have revolved halfway around the sun. Show in a sketch which end of Earth's axis will be tilted toward the sun.

Performance ▽ CHAPTER PROJECT 1 ▽ Assessment

Project Wrap Up Now you are ready to present your log, map, and drawings. Here are some ways you can graph your data: time of moonrise for each date; how often you saw the moon at each compass direction; how often you saw the moon at a specific time. Display your graphs. Discuss any patterns you discovered with your classmates. With your classmates, predict when and where you can see the moon.

Reflect and Record In your journal, write about the easiest and hardest parts of this project. What would you do differently if you observed the moon for another month? What observation(s) surprised you? Why?

Test Preparation
Use these questions to prepare for standardized tests.

Study the diagram. Then answer Questions 27–30. Numbers 1, 2, 3, and 4 on the diagram indicate locations of the moon in its orbit around Earth.

27. About how much time does it take the moon to revolve once around Earth?
    a. one day
    b. 7 days
    c. 27 days
    d. one year

28. Which of the following phases is the moon in at location 1?
    a. new   b. crescent
    c. half   d. full

29. At which location(s) could a lunar eclipse occur?
    a. 1 only   b. 3 only
    c. 1 and 3   d. 2 and 4

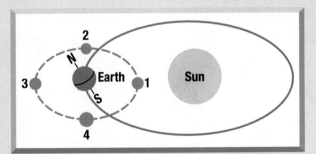

30. Only one side of the moon is visible from earth because
    a. the moon does not rotate on its axis.
    b. the moon does not revolve around Earth.
    c. the moon is in a geosynchronous orbit around Earth.
    d. the moon revolves once and rotates once in the same period of time.

The Solar System

This artist's conception shows the *Cassini* space probe arriving near Saturn's rings in 2004.

WEB ACTIVITY
www.phschool.com

2

Model of the Solar System

If you could drive from Earth to the sun at 100 kilometers per hour, your trip would take 170 years. And most distances in the solar system are even greater! The *Cassini* space probe left Earth for Saturn in 1997 traveling much faster than highway speed, but will not arrive at Saturn's rings until 2004. Sizes in the solar system can be huge, too. Compared with some of the other planets in the solar system, Earth is very small. Saturn, for example, is about 10 times Earth's diameter.

In this chapter, you will get to know many of the objects in the solar system. To help you understand the huge distances and sizes, you will design three different scale models of the solar system.

Your Goal To design scale models of the solar system.

To complete this project, you will
- design a model to show the planets' distances from the sun
- design a model to show the planets' sizes relative to the sun
- test different scales to see if you can use the same scale for both size and distance in one model

Get Started Begin by previewing the tables with distances and diameters on pages 63 and 71. Brainstorm with a group of classmates how you will build your models. Prepare a data sheet to record your calculations of scaled-down distances and diameters.

Check Your Progress You will be working on this project as you study this chapter. To keep your project on track, look for Check Your Progress boxes at the following points.

Section 1 Review, page 55: Design a model to show distances.
Section 3 Review, page 69: Design a model to show diameters.
Section 4 Review, page 77: Design one scale model that shows both sizes and distances.

Wrap Up At the end of the chapter (page 91), you will present your design to the class.

SECTION

1 Observing the Solar System

DISCOVER ··········································

How Do Mass and Speed Affect an Object's Motion?

1. Have your partner push a toy truck across the table toward you. Stop the truck with your hands.

2. Repeat Step 1, but have your partner push the truck a little faster. Was it easier or harder to stop the truck than in Step 1?

3. Now add some rocks or other heavy objects to the truck and repeat Step 1. Your partner should push the truck at the same speed as in Step 1. How hard was it to stop the truck this time compared to Step 1?

4. Repeat Step 2 with the rocks still in the truck. How hard was it to stop the truck this time?

Think It Over
Predicting How hard would it be to stop the truck if your partner pushed it more slowly? If you added more mass to the truck?

GUIDE FOR READING

◆ How do the heliocentric and geocentric descriptions of the solar system differ?

◆ What did Kepler discover about the orbits of the planets?

◆ What two factors keep the planets in their orbits?

Reading Tip As you read, make a list of the evidence that supports the heliocentric system.

Have you ever lain outdoors on a starry night, gazing up at the stars? As you watch, the stars seem to move across the sky. The sky seems to be rotating right over your head. In fact, from the Northern Hemisphere, the sky appears to rotate completely around Polaris, the North Star, once every 24 hours.

Now think about what you see every day. During the day, the sun appears to move across the sky. From here on Earth, it seems as if Earth is stationary and that the sun, moon, and stars are all moving around Earth. But is the sky really moving above you? Centuries ago, before there were space shuttles or even telescopes, there was no easy way to find out.

Figure 1 This photo was made by exposing the camera film for several hours. Each star appears as part of a circle, and all the stars seem to revolve around a single point.

Wandering Stars

When the ancient Greeks watched the stars move across the sky, they noticed that the patterns of most of the stars didn't change. Although the stars seemed to move, they stayed in the same position relative to each other. For example, the constellations kept the same shapes from night to night and from year to year.

As they observed the sky more carefully, the Greeks noticed something surprising. Five points of light seemed to wander among the stars. The Greeks called these objects *planets*, from the Greek word meaning "wandering star." The Greeks made very careful observations of the motions of the five planets they could see. You know these planets by the names the ancient Romans later gave them: Mercury, Venus, Mars, Jupiter, and Saturn.

Greek Ideas: Earth at the Center

When you look up at the sky, you can almost imagine that you are under a rotating dome with the stars pasted on it. The Greeks thought that they were inside a rotating dome they called the celestial sphere. Most Greek astronomers believed that the universe is perfect and unchangeable and that Earth is stationary in the center of the celestial sphere. Since *geo* is the Greek word for Earth, an Earth-centered explanation is known as a **geocentric** (jee oh SEN trik) system. **In a geocentric system, Earth is at the center of the revolving planets.**

In A.D. 140, the Greek astronomer Ptolemy (TAHL uh mee) explained the motion of the planets in another way. Like the earlier Greeks, Ptolemy thought that Earth is at the center of the system of planets. Ptolemy also thought that the moon, Mercury, Venus, the sun, Mars, Jupiter, and Saturn revolve around Earth.

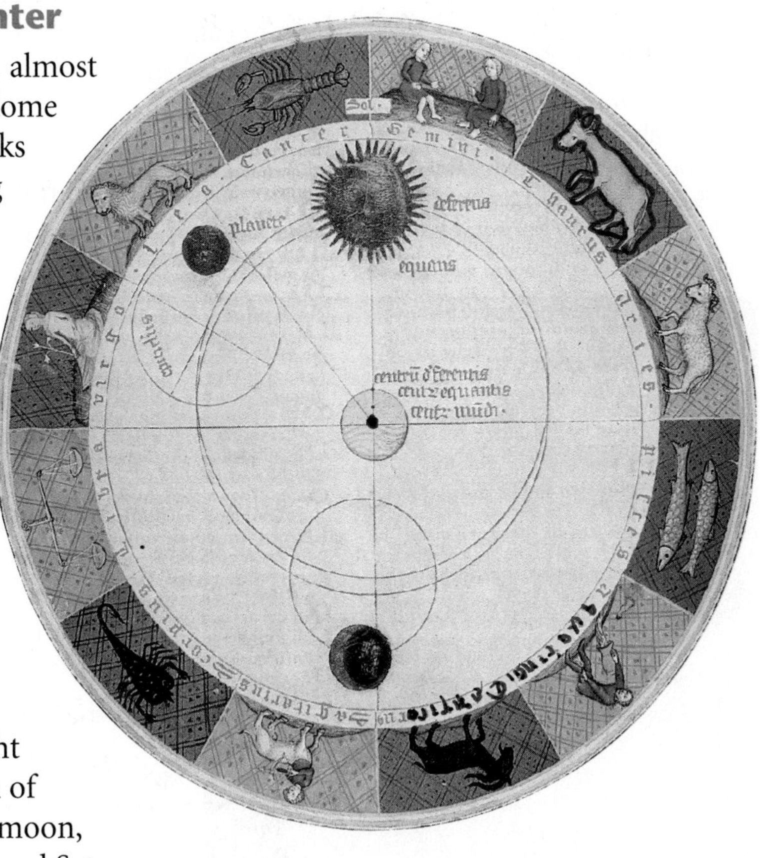

In Ptolemy's explanation, however, the planets move on little circles that move on bigger circles. Ptolemy thought that this explained why the planets seem to move at different speeds, and even backwards, among the stars. For the next 1,400 years, people believed that Ptolemy's ideas were correct.

Figure 2 In the 1500s, an astronomy book published this illustration of Ptolemy's system. *Interpreting Diagrams* *Where is Earth located in this illustration?*

✓ *Checkpoint* *What is a geocentric system?*

Copernicus's Idea: Sun at the Center

In the early 1500s, the Polish astronomer Nicolaus Copernicus developed another explanation for the motions of the planets. Copernicus thought that the sun is at the center of the system of planets. His sun-centered system is called a **heliocentric** (hee lee oh SEN trik) system. *Helios* is Greek for "sun." **In a heliocentric system, Earth and the other planets revolve around the sun.** Copernicus's explanation included the six planets he knew about: Mercury, Venus, Earth, Mars, Jupiter, and Saturn.

Galileo's Observations

In the 1500s and 1600s, most people still believed Ptolemy's geocentric explanation. However, the Italian astronomer Galileo Galilei, who lived nearly 100 years after Copernicus, thought that the heliocentric explanation was correct.

Recall from Chapter 1 that Galileo was the first scientist to use a telescope to look at objects in the sky. With his telescope, Galileo made two discoveries that supported the heliocentric model. First, Galileo saw four moons revolving around Jupiter. Galileo's observations of Jupiter's moons showed that not everything in the sky revolves around Earth.

Figure 3 From this observatory, Tycho Brahe made accurate observations of the planets for nearly 20 years. His data became the basis for many important discoveries.

Galileo's observations of Venus also supported Copernicus's heliocentric system. Galileo discovered that Venus goes through phases similar to those of Earth's moon. Galileo reasoned that the phases of Venus could not be explained if Earth were at the center of the system of planets. So Ptolemy's geocentric system could not be correct.

Galileo's evidence gradually convinced others that Copernicus's explanation was correct. Today, people talk about the "solar system" rather than the "Earth system." This shows that people accept Copernicus's idea that the sun is at the center.

✓ Checkpoint *What two discoveries made by Galileo supported the heliocentric description of the solar system?*

Brahe and Kepler

Copernicus and Galileo had correctly identified the sun as the center of the system of planets. But Copernicus, like Ptolemy, assumed that the orbits of the planets are circles.

Copernicus's ideas were based on observations made by the ancient Greeks. In the late 1500s, Tycho Brahe (TEE koh BRAH uh), a Danish astronomer, made much more accurate observations. Brahe carefully observed the positions of the planets for almost 20 years.

In 1600, a German mathematician, Johannes Kepler, went to work analyzing Brahe's data. Kepler tried to figure out the shape of the planets' orbits. At first, he assumed that the orbits are circles. When Kepler tried to figure out the exact orbit of Mars, however, no circle fit the observations.

Kepler had discovered that the orbit of each planet is an ellipse. An **ellipse** is an elongated circle, or oval shape. Kepler found that if he assumed that Mars's orbit is an ellipse, his calculations fit Brahe's observations better.

Inertia and Gravity

Kepler had discovered the correct shape of the planets' orbits. But he could not explain why the planets stay in orbit. The work of the English scientist Isaac Newton provided the answer to that puzzle. **Newton concluded that two factors—inertia and gravity—combine to keep the planets in orbit.**

Galileo had discovered that a moving object will continue to move until some force acts to stop its motion. This tendency of a moving object to continue in a straight line or a stationary object to remain in place is the object's **inertia.** The more mass an object has, the more inertia it has. As you found if you did the Discover activity, an object with greater inertia is more difficult to start or stop.

Isaac Newton picked up where Galileo had left off. Late in his life, Newton told the story of how watching an apple fall from a tree in 1665 had made him think about motion. He hypothesized that the same force that pulls the apple to the ground also pulls the moon toward Earth. This force, called gravity, attracts all

A Loopy Ellipse

You can draw an ellipse.

1. 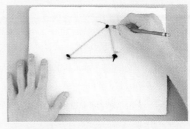 Carefully stick two pushpins about 10 cm apart through a sheet of white paper on top of corrugated cardboard.

2. Tie the ends of a 30-cm piece of string together. Place the string around the pushpins.

3. Keeping the string tight, move a pencil around inside the string.

4. Now place the pushpins 5 cm apart. Repeat Step 3.

Predicting How does changing the distance between the pushpins affect the ellipse's shape? What shape would you draw if you used only one pushpin?

Figure 4 Newton was a man of many achievements. Among them was the invention of this telescope.

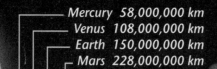

Mercury 58,000,000 km
Venus 108,000,000 km
Earth 150,000,000 km
Mars 228,000,000 km

Jupiter
778,000,000 km

Saturn
1,427,000,000 km

objects toward each other. The strength of gravity depends on the masses of the objects and the distance between them.

Newton figured out that Earth keeps pulling the moon toward it with gravity. At the same time, the moon keeps moving ahead because of its inertia. Earth curves away as the moon falls toward it, so the moon winds up in orbit around Earth.

In the same way, the planets are in orbit around the sun because the sun's gravity pulls on them while their inertia keeps them moving ahead. Therefore, the planets keep moving around the sun and end up in orbit.

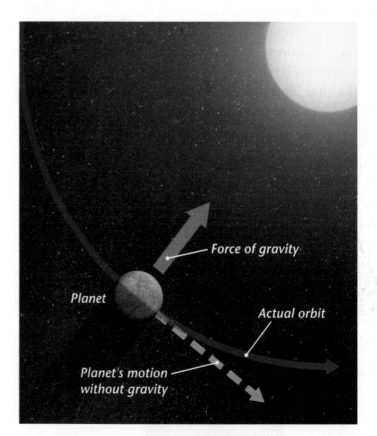

Figure 5 If there were no force of gravity, inertia would make a planet travel in a straight line. But because gravity pulls the planet toward the sun, the planet actually travels in an elliptical orbit around the sun.
Interpreting Diagrams What would happen if a planet had no inertia?

Force of gravity

Planet

Actual orbit

Planet's motion without gravity

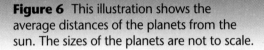

Uranus
2,871,000,000 km

Neptune
4,497,000,000 km

Pluto
5,913,000,000 km

Figure 6 This illustration shows the average distances of the planets from the sun. The sizes of the planets are not to scale.

More to Discover

Since Newton's time, our knowledge about the solar system has increased dramatically. Newton knew of the same six planets the ancient Greeks had known—Mercury, Venus, Earth, Mars, Jupiter, and Saturn. Now astronomers know three more planets—Uranus, Neptune, and Pluto. Astronomers have also identified many other objects in the solar system, such as comets and asteroids, that you will learn about later in this chapter.

Galileo and Newton used telescopes on Earth to observe the solar system. Astronomers still use telescopes on Earth, but they have also made close-up observations of the planets from space probes sent far into the solar system. Our understanding of the solar system continues to change every day. Who knows what new discoveries will be made in your lifetime!

Section 1 Review

1. How is Copernicus's description of the system of planets different from Ptolemy's description?
2. How did Galileo's observations of Jupiter's moons help to show that the geocentric explanation is incorrect?
3. What shape are the orbits of the planets? How was the discovery of this orbit shape made?
4. What two factors act together to keep the planets in orbit around the sun?
5. **Thinking Critically Applying Concepts** People usually say that the sun rises in the east, moves across the sky, and sets in the west. Is this description literally correct? Explain.

Check Your Progress

CHAPTER PROJECT 2

Begin by making a table that shows the distances of the planets from the sun. To help visualize the solar system, you can reduce all the distances by the same amount: for example, divide all distances by 100,000 or 1,000,000. You can use the resulting smaller numbers to design a scale model of the solar system. Record your calculations on your data sheet. Now choose a different scale and repeat your calculations. Which scale makes it easier to see the relative distances between the planets and the sun?

SECTION

2 The Sun

DISCOVER • ACTIVITY • • • •

How Can You Safely Observe the Sun?

1. Clamp a pair of binoculars to a ring stand.

2. Cut a hole in a 20-cm by 28-cm sheet of thin cardboard so that it will fit over the binoculars, as shown in the photo. The cardboard should cover one lens, but allow light through the other lens. Tape the cardboard on securely. **CAUTION:** *Never look directly at the sun. You will hurt your eyes if you do.*

3. Use the binoculars to project an image of the sun onto a sheet of white paper. The cardboard will shade the white paper. Change the focus and move the paper back and forth until you get a sharp image.

Think It Over

Observing Draw what you see on the paper. What do you see on the surface of the sun?

GUIDE FOR READING

◆ How does the sun get its energy?

◆ What are the layers of the sun's atmosphere?

◆ What are some features of the sun's surface?

Reading Tip As you read, write a sentence defining each boldfaced term in your own words.

The sun's gravity is by far the most powerful force in the solar system—strong enough to hold all of the planets and comets in orbit! The sun's gravity is so strong because the sun's mass is very large. In fact, 99.8 percent of the mass of the solar system is in the sun.

Like Earth, the sun has an interior and an atmosphere. Unlike Earth, however, the sun does not have a solid surface. The sun is a ball of glowing gas. About three fourths of the sun's mass is hydrogen, one fourth is helium, and very small amounts are other chemical elements.

The Sun's Interior

The interior of the sun is like a giant furnace. Like furnaces in houses, the sun produces energy. But the sun does not get its energy from burning fuels such as oil. **Instead, the sun's energy comes from nuclear fusion.** In the process of **nuclear fusion,** hydrogen atoms join together to form helium. Nuclear fusion occurs only under conditions of extremely high temperature and pressure. The temperature inside the sun's **core,** or center, reaches about 15 million degrees Celsius, high enough for nuclear fusion to occur.

The total mass of the helium produced by nuclear fusion is slightly less than the total mass of the hydrogen that goes into it. The change in mass occurs because some of the matter is converted into energy, including light and heat. The light and heat gradually move from the core of the sun to its atmosphere and escape into space. Some of this light and heat reach Earth, becoming Earth's main source of energy.

There is enough hydrogen fuel in the core of the sun to last for a total of 10 billion years. The sun is now only about 5 billion years old, so you don't have to worry about the sun "burning out" any time soon!

☑ *Checkpoint* *Where in the sun does nuclear fusion occur?*

The Sun's Atmosphere

The sun's atmosphere has three layers: the photosphere, the chromosphere, and the corona. There are no boundaries between the layers of the sun.

The Photosphere The inner layer of the sun's atmosphere is called the **photosphere** (FOH tuh sfeer). The Greek word *photo* means "light," so *photosphere* means the sphere that makes light. When you look at an image or photograph of the sun, you are looking at the photosphere.

The Chromosphere During a total solar eclipse, the moon blocks light from the photosphere. The photosphere no longer provides the glare that keeps you from seeing the sun's faint, outer layers. At the beginning and end of a total eclipse, you can see a reddish glow just around the photosphere. This glow comes from the middle layer of the sun's atmosphere, the **chromosphere.** The Greek word *chromo* means "color," so the chromosphere is the "color sphere."

The Corona In the middle of a total solar eclipse, the moon also blocks light from the chromosphere. At these times an even fainter layer of the sun becomes visible, as you can see in Figure 7. This outer layer, which looks like a white halo around the sun, is called the **corona,** which means "crown" in Latin. From Earth's surface, the corona is only visible during eclipses or from special telescopes. But astronomers can use telescopes in space to observe the corona all the time and to study how it changes.

Figure 7 During a total solar eclipse, you can see light from the corona, the outer layer of the sun's atmosphere. *Inferring Why is it easiest to photograph the sun's outer layers during a solar eclipse?*

The corona sends out a stream of electrically charged particles called **solar wind.** Normally Earth's atmosphere and magnetic field block these particles. However, near the North and South poles, the particles can enter Earth's atmosphere, where they hit gas molecules and cause them to glow. The result is rippling sheets of light in the sky called auroras.

☑ *Checkpoint* *During what event could you see the sun's corona?*

Features on the Sun

For hundreds of years, scientists have used telescopes to look at the sun. (To protect their eyes, they used a filter or projected the sun onto a white surface, as in the Discover activity.) The dark spots that they saw on the sun's surface became known as sunspots. The spots seemed to move across the sun's surface, which showed that the sun rotates on its axis, just as Earth does. **Features on or above the sun's surface include sunspots, prominences, and solar flares.**

Sunspots As you can see in Figure 8, sunspots look like small, dark areas on the sun's surface. But in fact, they can be as large as Earth. **Sunspots** are areas of gas on the sun that are cooler than the gases around them. Cooler gases don't give off as much light as hotter gases, which is why sunspots look darker than the rest of the photosphere.

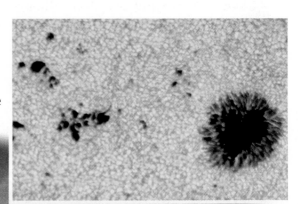

Figure 8 Sunspots are areas of gas on the sun that are cooler than the gas around them. Many of the sunspots in these photos are about as large as Earth.

The number of sunspots on the sun varies over a period of 10 or 11 years. Some scientists have hypothesized that short-term changes in climate on Earth may be related to sunspot cycles. Satellites have recently collected data that show that the amount of energy the sun produces changes slightly from year to year. Some scientists think that these increases and decreases, which may be linked to the number of sunspots, may cause changes in Earth's temperature. Scientists need to make more observations in order to test this hypothesis.

EXPLORING *the Sun*

The diameter of the sun (not including the chromosphere and the corona) is 1.4 million kilometers.

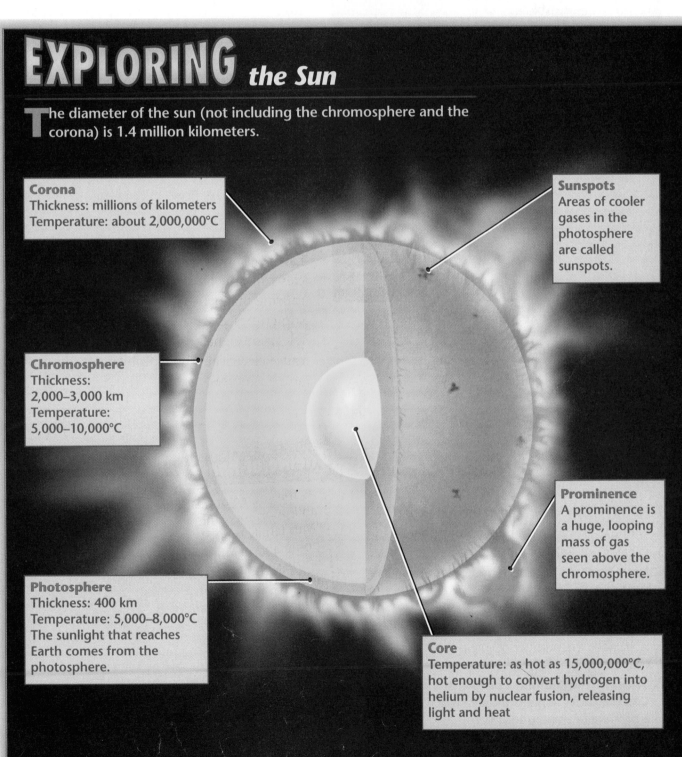

Corona
Thickness: millions of kilometers
Temperature: about 2,000,000°C

Sunspots
Areas of cooler gases in the photosphere are called sunspots.

Chromosphere
Thickness:
2,000–3,000 km
Temperature:
5,000–10,000°C

Prominence
A prominence is a huge, looping mass of gas seen above the chromosphere.

Photosphere
Thickness: 400 km
Temperature: 5,000–8,000°C
The sunlight that reaches Earth comes from the photosphere.

Core
Temperature: as hot as 15,000,000°C, hot enough to convert hydrogen into helium by nuclear fusion, releasing light and heat

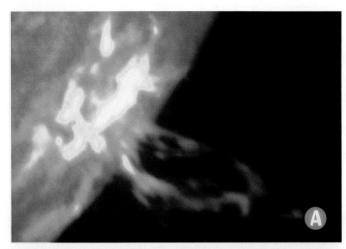

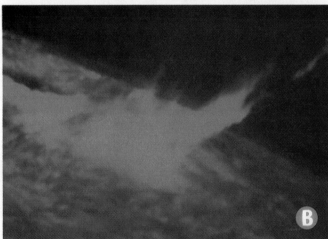

Figure 9 A. Prominences are huge loops of gas that connect different parts of sunspot regions. **B.** Solar flares on the sun release large amounts of energy. *Relating Cause and Effect How can solar flares affect communications on Earth?*

Prominences Sunspots usually occur in pairs or groups. Reddish loops of gas called **prominences** link different parts of sunspot regions. When a group of sunspots is near the edge of the sun as seen from Earth, these loops can stick out over the edge of the sun. If an eclipse hides the sun's photosphere, astronomers are able to see these loops. Prominences are about the same temperature as the sun's chromosphere, about 10,000 degrees Celsius.

Solar Flares Sometimes the loops in sunspot regions suddenly connect, releasing large amounts of energy. The energy heats gas on the sun to millions of degrees Celsius, causing the hydrogen gas to explode out into space. These explosions are known as **solar flares.**

Solar flares can greatly increase the solar wind from the corona, resulting in an increase in the number of particles reaching Earth's atmosphere. These solar wind particles can affect Earth's upper atmosphere, causing magnetic storms. Magnetic storms sometimes disrupt radio, telephone, and television signals. Magnetic storms can also cause electrical power problems for homes and businesses.

Section 2 Review

1. How is energy produced in the sun's core?
2. Name the layers of the sun's atmosphere.
3. What is the solar wind?
4. Describe three features found on or above the surface of the sun.
5. Why do sunspots look darker than the rest of the sun's photosphere?
6. How does the number of sunspots change over time?
7. **Thinking Critically Comparing and Contrasting** What is the difference between a prominence and a solar flare?

Science at Home

As the source of heat and light, the sun is an important symbol in many cultures. With family members, look around your home and neighborhood for illustrations of the sun on signs, flags, clothing, and in artwork. Which parts of the sun's atmosphere do the illustrations show? Describe the layers of the sun's atmosphere to your family.

STORMY SUNSPOTS

Problem

How are magnetic storms on Earth related to sunspot activity?

Skills Focus

graphing, interpreting data

Materials

graph paper   pencil   straightedge

Procedure

1. Use the data in the table to make a line graph of sunspot activity between 1967 and 1997.
2. On the graph, label the x-axis "Year." Use a scale with 2-year intervals, from 1967 to 1997.
3. Label the y-axis "Sunspot Number." Use a scale of 0 through 160 in intervals of 10.
4. Graph a point for the Sunspot Number for each year.
5. Complete your graph by drawing lines to connect the points.

Sunspots			
Year	Sunspot Number	Year	Sunspot Number
1967	93.8	1983	66.6
1969	105.0	1985	17.9
1971	66.6	1987	29.4
1973	38.0	1989	157.6
1975	15.5	1991	145.7
1977	27.5	1993	54.6
1979	155.4	1995	17.5
1981	140.4	1997	23.4

Analyze and Conclude

1. Based on your graph, which years had the highest Sunspot Number? The lowest Sunspot Number?
2. How often does the cycle of maximum and minimum activity repeat?
3. When was the most recent maximum sunspot activity? The most recent minimum sunspot activity?
4. Compare your sunspot graph with the magnetic storms graph. What relationship can you infer between periods of high sunspot activity and magnetic storms? Explain.
5. **Apply** During which years do you think electrical disturbances on Earth were most common?

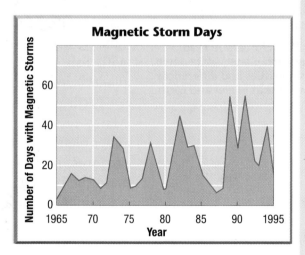

More to Explore

Using the pattern of sunspot activity you found, predict the number of peaks you would expect in the next 30 years. Around which years would you expect the peaks to occur?

ACTIVITY

How Does Mars Look From Earth?

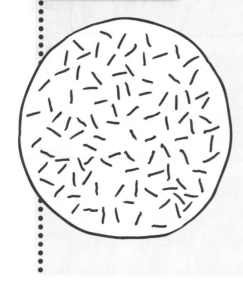

1. Work in pairs. On a sheet of paper, draw a circle 20 cm across to represent Mars. Draw about 100 small lines, each about 1 cm long, at random places inside the circle.

2. Have your partner look at your drawing of Mars from the other side of the room. Your partner should draw what he or she sees.

3. Compare your original drawing with what your partner drew. Then look at your own drawing from across the room.

Think It Over

Observing Did your partner draw any connecting lines that were not actually on your drawing? What can you conclude about the accuracy of descriptions of other planets as observed from Earth?

Where could you find a planet whose surface is hot enough to melt lead? How about a planet whose atmosphere has almost entirely leaked away? And how about a planet with volcanoes higher than any on Earth? Finally, what about a planet with oceans of water brimming with fish and other life? These are descriptions of the four planets closest to the sun, known as the inner planets

Earth and the other three inner planets—Mercury, Venus, and Mars—are more similar to each other than they are to the five outer planets. **The four inner planets are small and have rocky surfaces.** These planets are often called the **terrestrial planets,** from the Latin word *terra*, which means "Earth." Figure 10 gives a summary of information about the inner planets.

Earth

Our planet's atmosphere extends more than 100 kilometers above Earth's surface. The oxygen you need to live makes up about 20 percent of the gases in Earth's atmosphere. Almost all the rest is nitrogen gas, with small amounts of argon and other gases. Earth's atmosphere also contains water vapor and clouds of water droplets. From space, astronauts can usually see past the clouds to Earth's surface.

Most of Earth, about 70 percent, is covered with water. Perhaps the planet should be named "Water" instead of "Earth"! No other planet in our solar system has oceans like Earth's.

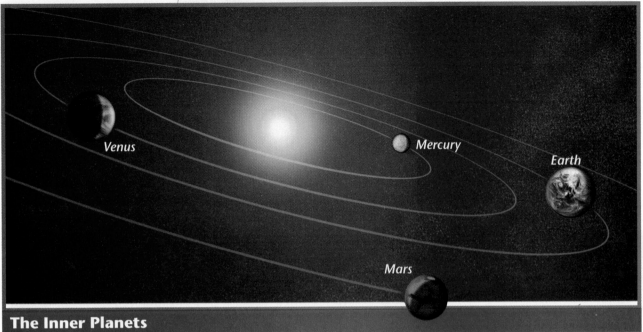

The Inner Planets

Planet	Diameter (kilometers)	Period of Rotation (Earth days)	Average Distance From the Sun (kilometers)	Period of Revolution (Earth years)	Number of Moons
Mercury	4,878	59	58,000,000	0.24	0
Venus	12,104	243	108,000,000	0.62	0
Earth	12,756	1	150,000,000	1	1
Mars	6,794	1.03	228,000,000	1.9	2

Figure 10 The inner planets take up only a small part of the solar system. The diameter of the entire solar system is more than 25 times the diameter of Mars's orbit.

INTEGRATING EARTH SCIENCE As you can see in Figure 11, Earth has three main layers—a crust, a mantle, and a core. The crust includes the solid rocky surface. Under the crust is the mantle, a layer of hot molten rock. When volcanoes erupt, this hot material rises to the surface. Earth has a dense inner core made up mainly of iron and nickel. The outer core is liquid, but the inner core is probably solid.

Scientists have been studying Earth for many years. They use what they know about Earth to make inferences about the other planets. For example, when astronomers find volcanoes on other planets, they infer that these planets have or once had hot material inside them. As we continue to learn more about our own planet, scientists will be able to apply that new knowledge to the study of the other planets.

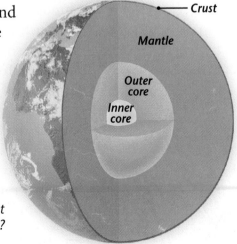

Crust

Mantle

Outer core

Inner core

Figure 11 Earth has a solid, rocky surface. *Interpreting Diagrams What are Earth's three main layers?*

Figure 12 This photo of Mercury and the closeup view of some of its craters (inset) were taken by the *Mariner 10* space probe.

Mercury

The planet closest to the sun is Mercury. Mercury is not much larger than Earth's moon and has no moons of its own. Astronomers have been able to infer that the interior of Mercury is made up mainly of the dense metals iron and nickel.

Exploring Mercury Because Mercury is so close to the sun, people on Earth never get a good view of Mercury. Much of the knowledge that astronomers have about Mercury's surface came from a single probe, *Mariner 10.* It flew by three times in 1974 and 1975. *Mariner 10* photographed only half of Mercury's surface, so astronomers still don't know much about what the rest of Mercury is like.

Mariner 10's photographs show that, like the moon, Mercury has many flat plains and many craters on its surface. The craters on Mercury have been named for artists, writers, and musicians, including the composers Bach and Mozart.

Mercury's Atmosphere Mercury has an extremely thin atmosphere. Apparently the gases Mercury once had were heated so much that the gas particles moved very fast. Since they were moving so fast, the gas particles escaped from Mercury's weak gravity into space. However, astronomers have detected small amounts of sodium and other gases in Mercury's atmosphere.

Mercury is a planet of extremes. It is so close to the sun that during the day, the side facing the sun reaches temperatures of 430°C. Because Mercury has almost no atmosphere, at night all the heat escapes into space. The temperature drops to −170°C. Mercury thus has a greater range of temperatures than any other planet in the solar system.

✓ *Checkpoint* *Why is it difficult for astronomers to learn about Mercury?*

Venus

Whenever you see a bright object in the west after sunset, it is probably Venus. When Venus shines brightly like that, it is known as the "evening star," though of course it really isn't a star. Stars shine with their own light, while Venus shines because it is reflecting light from the sun, just as the other planets and moons do. At other times, you see Venus rise before the sun in the morning. It is then known as the "morning star." At still other times, Venus is too close to the sun in the sky for you to see it from Earth.

Venus is so similar in size to Earth that it is sometimes called Earth's twin. Astronomers also think that the density and internal structure of Venus are similar to Earth's. However, in many other ways, Venus is very different from Earth.

Venus's Rotation Venus takes about 7.5 Earth months to revolve around the sun. It takes about 8 months for Venus to rotate on its axis. Venus rotates so slowly that its "day" is longer than its "year." Oddly, Venus rotates from east to west, the opposite direction from most other planets and moons. This type of rotation is called **retrograde rotation,** from the Latin words for "moving backward." One hypothesis proposed by astronomers to explain this unusual rotation is that Venus was struck by a very large object billions of years ago. Such a collision could have caused the direction of its rotation to change.

Sharpen your Skills

Graphing ACTIVITY

Using data in Figure 10 on page 63, make a line graph of the average distance from the sun and period of revolution of Mercury, Venus, Earth, and Mars. Describe how the two variables are related. If you wish, add data on Jupiter, Saturn, Uranus, Neptune, and Pluto from Figure 19 on page 71.

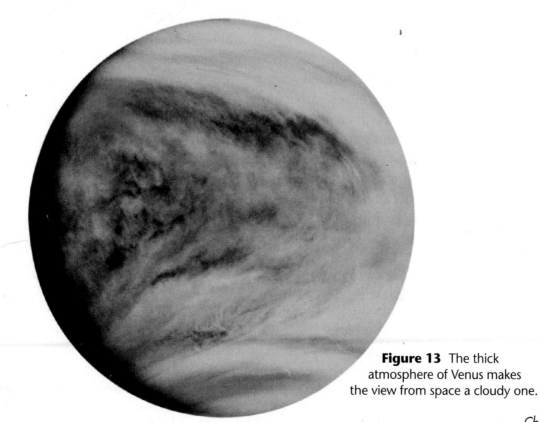

Figure 13 The thick atmosphere of Venus makes the view from space a cloudy one.

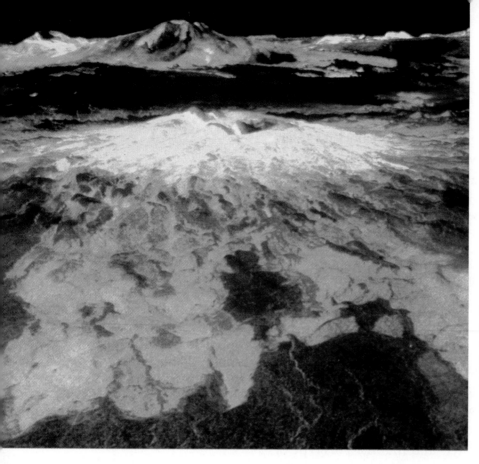

Figure 14 The *Magellan* spacecraft used radar to penetrate Venus's clouds. This three-dimensional image of a volcano on Venus was created by a computer using radar data. The height of the mountains is exaggerated to make them stand out.

Venus's Atmosphere The atmosphere of Venus is so thick that every day is a cloudy one. Venus never has a sunny day. From Earth, astronomers see only a smooth cloud cover over Venus all the time.

If you could stand on the surface of Venus, you would quickly be crushed by the weight of its atmosphere. The pressure of Venus's atmosphere is 90 times greater than the pressure of Earth's atmosphere. You could not breathe on Venus because its atmosphere is mostly carbon dioxide. Also, its clouds are partly made of sulfuric acid.

Because Venus is closer to the sun than Earth, it gets more solar energy than Earth does. Ordinary light from the sun can penetrate Venus's atmosphere and hit its surface. The surface heats up and then gives off heat. Carbon dioxide traps this heat in the atmosphere. So Venus's surface becomes hotter and hotter, until it is about 460°C—hot enough to melt lead. This trapping of heat by the atmosphere is called the **greenhouse effect.**

Exploring Venus A total of 19 spacecraft have visited Venus, more than have visited any other planet. Some have even penetrated its clouds and landed on its surface. The first spacecraft to land and send back information, *Venera 7,* landed in 1970 but survived for only 23 minutes. Later spacecraft were more durable and sent back pictures and other data from Venus's surface.

Scientists have learned most of what they know about Venus's surface from data collected by the *Magellan* probe. The *Magellan* probe reached Venus in 1990, carrying radar instruments. Radar works through clouds, so *Magellan* was able to map Venus's entire surface.

The *Magellan* views are so detailed that computers can be used to figure out what Venus would look like if you could fly just above its surface. Figure 14 shows one of these radar images. Venus is covered with rock, similar to many rocky areas on Earth. Venus has volcanoes with lava flows, many craters, and strange domes not found on other planets.

☑ *Checkpoint* **Why is the surface of Venus so hot?**

Mars

Mars is called the "red planet" because it has a slightly reddish tinge when you see it in the sky. The atmosphere of Mars is mostly carbon dioxide and has only 1 percent the pressure of Earth's atmosphere. You could walk around on Mars, but you would have to wear an airtight suit and carry your own air, like a scuba diver. Mars has clouds but they are very thin compared to the clouds on Earth.

Canals on Mars? In 1877, an Italian astronomer, Giovanni Schiaparelli (sky ah puh REL ee), announced that he had seen long, straight lines on Mars. He called them *canale,* or channels. In the 1890s and early 1900s, Percival Lowell, an American astronomer, convinced many people that these lines were canals that had been built by intelligent Martians to carry water. Astronomers now know that Lowell was mistaken. There are no canals on Mars.

Astronomers have found that some water remains on Mars in the form of ice at its north pole, as shown in Figure 15. During the winter, this polar ice cap is covered by a layer of frozen carbon dioxide. Mars' south pole has an ice cap made mostly of frozen carbon dioxide.

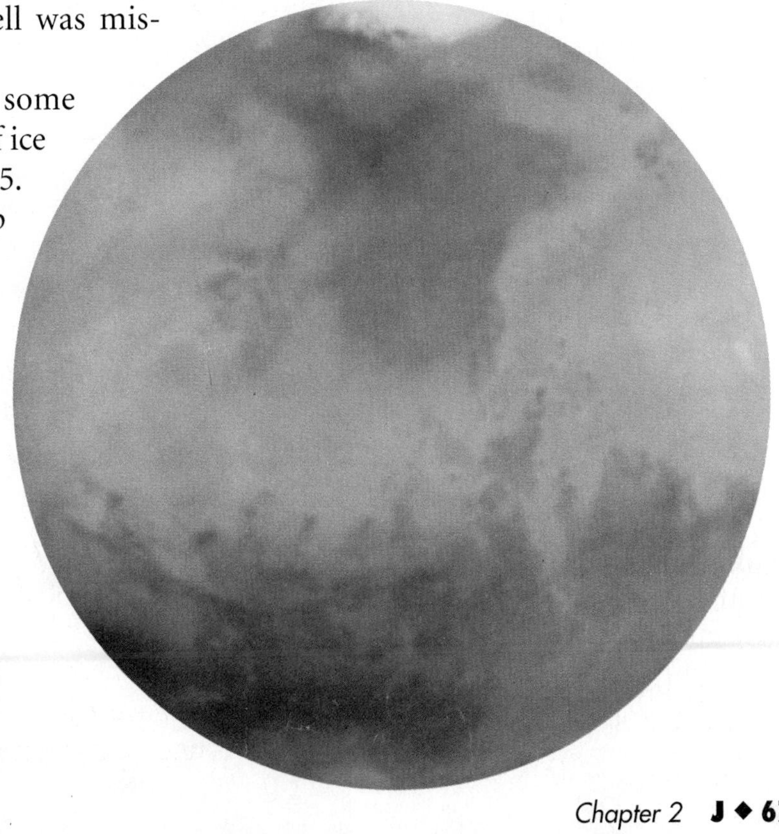

Figure 15 Because of its thin atmosphere and its distance from the sun, Mars is quite cold. Mars has ice caps at both poles.

Seasons on Mars Because the axis of Mars is tilted, Mars has seasons just as Earth does. As the seasons change on the dusty surface of Mars, wind storms arise and blow the dust around. Since the dust is blown off some regions, these regions look darker. A hundred years ago, some people thought these regions looked darker because plants were growing there. Astronomers now realize that it is just that wind storms blow dust off the surface.

Exploring Mars The United States has sent many spacecraft to Mars. The first ones, in the 1960s, seemed to show that Mars is barren and covered with craters like the moon. Later spacecraft showed that regions of Mars have giant volcanoes. Astronomers see signs that hot material flowed down the volcanoes in the past, but they don't think the volcanoes are active now.

In 1976, two NASA spacecraft, *Viking 1* and *Viking 2,* landed on Mars. They sent back close-up pictures from Mars's surface. The pictures showed that the rocks look red because they are covered with a rusty dust. Other parts of the *Viking* spacecraft went into orbit around Mars, sending back detailed pictures.

In 1997, *Mars Pathfinder* landed on Mars. As Figure 16 shows, close-up photographs from *Mars Pathfinder* show no oceans or even puddles of water. Photographs taken from space do show evidence that water flowed on Mars millions of years ago.

Figure 16 The surface of Mars is rugged and rocky. The object at the bottom of the photo is the *Mars Pathfinder* lander. You can see the remote-control rover *Sojourner* in the middle of the photo.

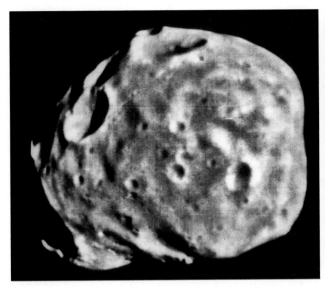

Figure 17 Phobos (left) and Deimos (right) are Mars's two small, crater-covered moons.

Mars Pathfinder carried a microwave-sized remote-control rover, called *Sojourner,* that investigated rocks on Mars. Also in 1997, another probe, *Mars Global Surveyor,* arrived in orbit around Mars, where it began mapping and photographing all of the planet's surface in detail.

Mars's Moons Mars has two very small moons. Phobos, the larger moon, is only 27 kilometers in diameter, about the distance a car can travel on the highway in 15 minutes. Deimos is even smaller, only 15 kilometers in diameter. Close-up views from space show that, like Earth's moon, Phobos and Deimos are covered with craters.

Section 3 Review

1. What features do all of the inner planets have in common?
2. What is Mercury's atmosphere like? Explain.
3. Why can astronomers see the surface of Mars clearly, but not the surface of Venus?
4. How have astronomers been able to study the surface of Venus?
5. What evidence do astronomers have that water once flowed on Mars?
6. **Thinking Critically Relating Cause and Effect** Venus is much farther from the sun than is Mercury. Yet temperatures on Venus are as high as those on the sunny side of Mercury. Explain why.

CHAPTER PROJECT 2

Check Your Progress
Now you will design a model that shows the relative diameters of the planets. Try several different scales to find one for which the smallest planet is clearly visible but the sun would still fit into your classroom. Convert the sun's and planets' diameters to scaled-down diameters and record your results on your data sheet. Compare your scaled-down diameters to objects you are familiar with, such as coins. Include your comparisons in your data sheet.

The Outer Planets

ACTIVITY

How Large Are the Outer Planets?

The table shows the diameters of the outer planets compared to Earth. For example, Jupiter's diameter is 11 times Earth's diameter.

1. Measure the diameter of a quarter in millimeters. This represents Earth's diameter. Trace the quarter to represent Earth.

2. If Earth were the size of a quarter, calculate how large Jupiter would be. Now draw a circle to represent Jupiter.

3. Repeat Step 2 for each of the other outer planets.

Think It Over

Classifying List the planets in order from largest to smallest. What is the largest outer planet? Which outer planet is much smaller than Earth?

Planet Diameters	
Planet	**Diameter**
Earth	1
Jupiter	11
Saturn	9.4
Uranus	4.0
Neptune	3.9
Pluto	0.17

GUIDE FOR READING

◆ What are the main characteristics of the gas giant planets?

◆ How is Pluto different from the other outer planets?

Reading Tip Before you read, preview the photos and captions in this section. Then write down any questions you have. Look for answers as you read.

Most of what astronomers know about the outer planets has come from visits by NASA space probes. *Voyager 1* and *Voyager 2* reached Jupiter in 1979 and sent back close-up views of the planet. *Voyager 1* went on to visit Saturn in 1980. *Voyager 2* also visited Saturn, but then moved on to explore Uranus and Neptune. In 1995, the spacecraft *Galileo* reached Jupiter and dropped a probe into Jupiter's atmosphere.

Structure of the Gas Giants

Compared to Earth, some planets are huge. The largest planet, Jupiter, has a diameter that is 11 times Earth's diameter. Jupiter's mass is more than 300 times Earth's mass. If you could put Earth next to Jupiter, Earth would look like a tiny Chihuahua next to an enormous Great Dane. If Earth were the height of an average student, Jupiter would be as tall as a six-story building.

Jupiter and the other planets farthest from the sun, as seen in Figure 19, are called the outer planets. **The first four outer planets—Jupiter, Saturn, Uranus, and Neptune—are much larger than Earth, and do not have solid surfaces.** Because these four planets are all so large, they are also called the **gas giants.** The fifth outer planet, Pluto, is small and rocky like the terrestrial planets.

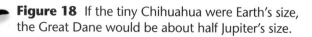

Figure 18 If the tiny Chihuahua were Earth's size, the Great Dane would be about half Jupiter's size.

The Outer Planets					
Planet	**Diameter (kilometers)**	**Period of Rotation (Earth days)**	**Average Distance From the Sun (kilometers)**	**Period of Revolution (Earth years)**	**Number of Moons**
Jupiter	142,800	0.41	778,000,000	12	18
Saturn	120,540	0.43	1,427,000,000	29	18
Uranus	51,200	0.72	2,871,000,000	84	20
Neptune	49,500	0.67	4,497,000,000	165	8
Pluto	2,200	6.4	5,913,000,000	248	1

Figure 19 The outer planets are much farther apart than the inner planets. At this scale, the inner planets are so small and close to the sun that they cannot be shown. *Observing Which outer planet is closest to the sun?*

Atmospheres Because the gas giants have so much mass, they exert a much stronger gravitational force than the terrestrial planets. The strong gravity keeps the giant planets' gases from escaping, so they have deep atmospheres. The composition of their atmospheres is similar to the gases in the sun. They are, on average, about 75 percent hydrogen, 24 percent helium, and 1 percent other elements.

None of the giant planets has a solid surface. If you could parachute into Jupiter's atmosphere, you would sink into denser and denser gas. You would be crushed by the enormous pressure long before you got to the center, or core, of the planet.

Solid Cores Astronomers think that each of the giant planets has a partly solid core made of rock, ice, frozen carbon dioxide, and other compounds. Each of these cores may have several times as much mass as Earth. But they are buried so deep inside the planets that it has been hard to find out much about them.

☑ *Checkpoint* *Why do the gas giants have large atmospheres?*

Jupiter

Jupiter is the most massive planet. In fact, Jupiter is more than 300 times as massive as Earth.

Jupiter's Atmosphere Like all of the gas giant planets, Jupiter has a thick atmosphere made up mainly of hydrogen and helium. Jupiter's atmosphere contains many colorful bands and swirls of thick clouds. An especially interesting feature in Jupiter's atmosphere is its Great Red Spot, a giant area of swirling clouds many times bigger than Earth. The Great Red Spot, shown in Figure 20, appears to be an ongoing storm similar to a hurricane on Earth.

Jupiter's Moons Recall that the astronomer Galileo discovered four of Jupiter's moons. These moons are named Io (EYE oh), Europa, Ganymede, and Callisto. These four moons are Jupiter's largest moons. Io, Ganymede, and Callisto are all larger than Earth's own moon. Since Galileo's time, astronomers have discovered more than a dozen additional moons revolving around Jupiter.

The *Voyager* and *Galileo* probes sent back images that showed detailed views of many of Jupiter's moons. Jupiter's moons are very different from one another, as you can see in Figure 21.

Figure 20 The larger photo of Jupiter was taken by the *Voyager 1* spacecraft. The small objects in front of Jupiter are two of Jupiter's moons, Io (left) and Europa (right). The Great Red Spot, shown in the inset, is a giant storm much larger in size than Earth.

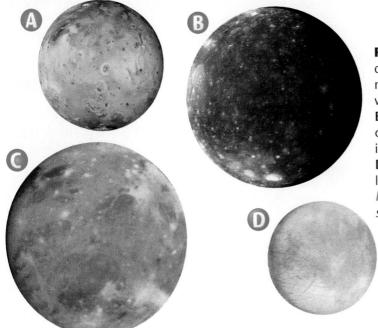

Figure 21 The astronomer Galileo discovered Jupiter's four largest moons. **A.** Io's surface is covered with large, active volcanoes. **B.** Callisto's surface is icy and covered with craters. **C.** Ganymede is the largest of Jupiter's moons. **D.** Europa's icy crust may have liquid water underneath.
Inferring Why was Galileo able to see only Jupiter's largest moons?

Io is covered with volcanoes. Over a dozen huge volcanoes are erupting all the time, so Io's surface changes from year to year because of the flows of hot material. The sulfur in the flows gives a variety of colors to Io's surface. From space, Io looks like a giant pizza. Europa has an icy crust that may have liquid water underneath. You will learn more about Europa in Section 6.

Ganymede is the largest of Jupiter's moons and has about twice the mass of Earth's moon. Ganymede's surface is icy and partly covered with craters. Other parts of the surface show giant grooves in the ice. Callisto also has an icy surface. It is so heavily cratered that no part of its surface is free of craters.

✓ *Checkpoint* *What are Jupiter's four largest moons?*

Saturn

The second-largest planet in the solar system is Saturn. Saturn is slightly smaller than Jupiter, but including its beautiful rings it has a greater overall diameter. The *Voyager* probes showed that Saturn, like Jupiter, has a thick atmosphere made up mainly of hydrogen and helium. Saturn's atmosphere also contains clouds and storms, but they are less dramatic than those on Jupiter. Saturn is the only planet that is less dense than water.

Saturn's Rings When Galileo first looked at Saturn with a telescope, he could see that something was sticking out on the sides, but he didn't know what it was. A few decades later, another astronomer using a better telescope discovered that Saturn had rings around it. Astronomers later found that these rings are made of chunks of ice and rock, each traveling in its own orbit around Saturn.

Model Saturn

Here's how you can build a scale model of Saturn.

1. Use a plastic foam sphere 8 cm in diameter to represent Saturn.

2. Use an overhead transparency to represent Saturn's rings. Cut a circle 18 cm in diameter out of the transparency. Cut a hole 9 cm in diameter out of the center of the circle.

3. Stick five toothpicks into Saturn, spaced equally around its equator. Put the transparency on the toothpicks and tape it to them. Sprinkle baking soda on the transparency.

4. Use a peppercorn to represent Titan. Place the peppercorn 72 cm away from Saturn on the same plane as the rings.

Making Models What do the particles of baking soda represent?

Figure 22 Saturn's rings are made up of ice chunks and rocks of many different sizes. The smaller photo shows that there are actually many small rings. The colors in this photo have been added by a computer. *Observing Why might it be hard to see Saturn's rings when their edges are facing Earth?*

From Earth, it looks as though Saturn has only a few rings, and that they are divided from each other by narrow, dark regions. The *Voyager* spacecraft discovered that each of these obvious rings is divided into dozens of smaller rings. In all, Saturn has hundreds of rings.

Saturn's rings are broad and thin, like a compact disc. Sometimes the rings are tipped so that observers see them at an angle. Occasionally, they are on edge, and then, because they are so thin, astronomers can't see them at all.

In the last few decades, rings have been discovered around the other three gas giants as well. But the rings around Jupiter, Uranus, and Neptune are not as spectacular as Saturn's.

Saturn's Moons Saturn's largest moon, Titan, is larger than Earth's own moon. Titan was discovered in 1665 but was known only as a point of light until the *Voyagers* went by. The probes showed that Titan has an atmosphere so thick that little light can get through it. Astronomers studying Hubble Space Telescope images can barely see Titan's surface.

Four other moons of Saturn are each over 1,000 kilometers in diameter. They are named Tethys (TEE this), Iapetus (eye AP uh tus), Dione, and Rhea. *Voyager* images show craters and canyons on these moons.

Checkpoint **What are Saturn's rings made of?**

Figure 23 This image of Saturn and six of its moons combines photos taken by *Voyager 1* and *Voyager 2*.

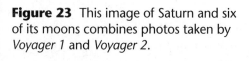

Uranus

Although the gas giant Uranus (YOOR uh nus) is about four times the diameter of Earth, it is still much smaller than Jupiter and Saturn. Uranus is twice as far from the sun as Saturn, so it is much colder. Uranus looks bluish because of traces of methane in its atmosphere.

Discovery of Uranus In 1781, Uranus became the first new planet discovered since ancient times. Astronomer William Herschel, in England, found an object in the sky that did not look like a star. At first he thought it might be a comet. But other astronomers soon calculated its orbit and realized that it was a planet beyond Saturn. The discovery made Herschel famous and started an era of solar system exploration.

Exploring Uranus In 1986, about 200 years after Herschel's discovery, *Voyager 2* arrived at Uranus and sent back our only close-up views of that giant planet. Images from *Voyager 2* show only a few clouds on Uranus's surface, but even these few allowed astronomers to calculate that Uranus rotates in about 17 hours.

Strangely, Uranus's axis is tilted at an angle of about 90° from the vertical, as shown in Figure 24. Viewed from Earth, Uranus is rotating from top to bottom instead of from side to side, the way most of the other planets do. Astronomers think that billions of years ago Uranus was hit by an object that knocked it on its side.

Uranus's Moons Photographs from *Voyager 2* showed that Uranus's five largest moons have icy, cratered surfaces. The craters show that the moons have been hit by rocks from space. Uranus's moons also have lava flows on their surfaces, suggesting that material has erupted from inside each moon. *Voyager 2* images revealed ten moons that had never been seen before. In 1999, astronomers discovered three more moons, for a total of 20.

Figure 24 A. This composite image of *Voyager 2* photos includes Uranus and five of its 20 moons. **B.** Unlike most other planets, Uranus rotates on its side.

Sun

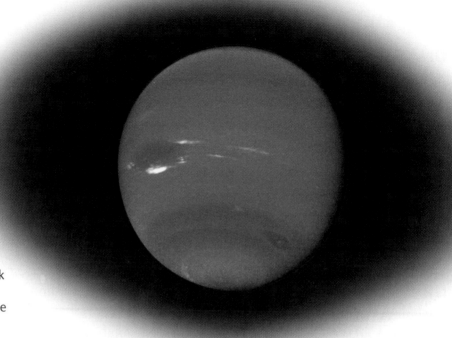

Figure 25 The Great Dark Spot was a giant storm in Neptune's atmosphere. The storm is now gone.

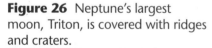

Figure 26 Neptune's largest moon, Triton, is covered with ridges and craters.

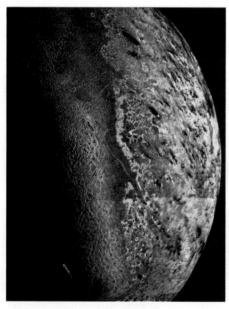

Neptune

Neptune is even farther from the sun than Uranus—in fact, it is 30 times Earth's distance from the sun. Unlike Uranus's nearly featureless blue atmosphere, Neptune's atmosphere contains visible clouds.

Discovery of Neptune The planet Neptune was discovered as a result of a mathematical prediction. Uranus was not quite following the orbit astronomers predicted for it. Astronomers hypothesized that there must be another, unseen planet whose gravity was affecting Uranus's orbit. By 1846, mathematicians in both England and France had calculated the orbit of this new planet. A few months later, an observer in Germany saw an unknown object in the sky. It was the new planet, now called Neptune.

Exploring Neptune In 1989 *Voyager 2* flew by Neptune, where it photographed a Great Dark Spot, as shown in Figure 25, about the size of Earth. Like the Great Red Spot on Jupiter, the Great Dark Spot probably was a giant storm. But the storm didn't last long. Images from the Hubble Space Telescope taken five years later showed that the Great Dark Spot was gone. Other, smaller spots and regions of clouds on Neptune seem to come and go.

Neptune's Moons Astronomers have discovered eight moons revolving around Neptune. Neptune's largest moon is Triton. The *Voyager* photos show that the region near Triton's south pole is covered with a cap of ice, and that dark material erupts from underneath.

☑ *Checkpoint* *Before they could see Neptune, what evidence led scientists to conclude that it existed?*

Pluto and Charon

Pluto and its single moon Charon are very different from the gas giants. **Pluto and Charon have solid surfaces and masses much less than that of Earth.** In fact, Pluto is less than two thirds the size of Earth's moon. Since Charon is more than half the size of Pluto, astronomers often consider them to be a double planet instead of a planet and a moon.

Pluto and Charon are so far from the sun that they revolve around the sun only once every 248 Earth years. Because Pluto and Charon are so small and far away, astronomers have been unable to learn much about them.

Discovery of Pluto and Charon The American astronomer Clyde Tombaugh discovered Pluto in 1930. He had been searching for a large object he thought might be affecting Neptune's orbit. Tombaugh spent 10 months looking at hundreds of thousands of images before he found Pluto. Charon was not discovered until 1978, by the astronomer James Christy. Christy was studying photographs of Pluto when he noticed that Pluto seemed to have a "bump." The bump turned out to be Charon.

Is Pluto Really a Planet? Pluto is so small that many astronomers do not think it should be called a planet at all. Pluto may be merely the largest of thousands of objects revolving around the sun out beyond Neptune. If astronomers had found these other objects before they found Pluto, they might not have called Pluto a planet.

Figure 27 The space between Pluto and Charon couldn't be clearly seen from Earth until 1999, when Pluto and Charon were observed with new telescopes. This photo, taken with the Hubble Space Telescope, clearly shows them as two objects. *Inferring Why do astronomers often call Pluto and Charon a double planet?*

Section 4 Review

1. How are the gas giants similar to each other? How are they different?
2. How is Pluto different from the gas giants?
3. What is the most prominent feature of Jupiter's surface? What causes this feature?
4. Why do astronomers think Uranus may have been hit by another object billions of years ago?
5. **Thinking Critically** Predicting Do you think astronomers have found all of the moons of the outer planets? Explain.

Check Your Progress

CHAPTER PROJECT 2

Once you have models that show size and distance separately, design another scale model of the solar system. This time, use the same scale for both size and distance. If your chalkboard is the sun, which planets would be in your classroom? Where would the other planets be with respect to your classroom, school grounds, and town?

Discuss with classmates any problems that would come up in building a model using the same scale for both size and distance. Revise your model as needed.

SPEEDING AROUND THE SUN

I n this lab, you will make and test a hypothesis about how a planet's distance from the sun is related to its period of revolution.

Problem

How does a planet's distance from the sun affect its period of revolution?

Materials

string, 1.5 m   one-hole rubber stopper
plastic tube, 6 cm   stopwatch
meter stick
weight or several washers

Procedure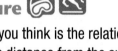

1. What do you think is the relationship between a planet's distance from the sun and its period of revolution? Write your hypothesis in the form of an "If . . . then . . ." statement.

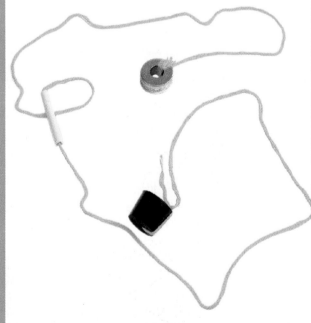

2. To test your hypothesis, you need to make a model planet.
   a. Thread the string through the rubber stopper hole. Tie the end of the string to the main part of the string. Pull tightly to make sure that the knot will not become untied.
   b. Thread the other end of the string through the plastic tube and tie a weight to that end. Have your teacher check both knots.
   c. Hold the plastic tube in your hand above your head. Swing the stopper around above your head. Practice keeping the stopper moving at a constant speed. The circle represents the planet's orbit. **CAUTION:** *Stand away from other students. Make sure the swinging stopper will not hit students or objects. Do not let go of the string.*

3. Before you try different distances for your model planet, copy the data table into your notebook.

DATA TABLE			
	Period of Revolution		
Distance (cm)	Trial 1	Trial 2	Trial 3	Average
20				
40				
60				

4. Pull the string so the stopper is 20 cm away from the plastic tube. Swing the stopper just fast enough to keep the stopper moving.

5. Have your partner time how long it takes for the stopper to make 10 revolutions. Divide by 10 to find the period of revolution. Record this number as Trial 1.

6. Repeat Steps 4–5 two more times. Record your results as Trials 2 and 3. Add the results of the three trials together and divide by three to find the average period of revolution.

7. If you pull the stopper out to 40 cm, do you think the period of revolution will increase or decrease? To find out, pull the stopper out to 40 cm and repeat Steps 4–6.

8. Based on your results in Step 7, do you want to revise your hypothesis? Make any needed changes. Then pull the stopper out to 60 cm and repeat Steps 4–6.

Analyze and Conclude

1. Which object in your model represented the sun? Which represented the planet?

2. What force did the pull on the string represent?

3. When you pulled the stopper out to make the orbit larger, did the string then represent a stronger or weaker force of gravity? Why?

4. What happened to the period of revolution when you made the orbit larger in Steps 7 and 8?

5. Did your observations support your hypothesis? Summarize your conclusions based on your observations.

6. Which planets take less time to revolve around the sun—those closer to the sun or those farther away? Use the model to support your answer.

7. **Think About It** What information did you consider when you made your hypothesis? How did having some experimental data help you modify your hypothesis?

Design an Experiment

Write a hypothesis relating the mass of a planet to its period of revolution. Then, using a stopper with a different mass, modify the activity to test your hypothesis. Before you swing the stopper, have your teacher check your knots.

SECTION

5 Comets, Asteroids, and Meteors

DISCOVER ·· ACTIVITY ····

Which Way Do Comet Tails Point?

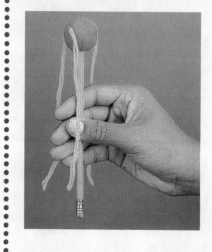

1. Form a small ball out of modeling clay to represent a comet.

2. Using a pencil point, push three 10-cm lengths of string into the ball. The strings represent the comet's tail. Stick the ball onto the pencil point, as shown in the photo.

3. Hold the ball about 1 m in front of a fan. The air from the fan represents the solar wind. Move the ball toward the fan, away from the fan, and from side to side.
CAUTION: *Keep your fingers away from the fan blades.*

Think It Over

Inferring How does moving the ball affect the direction in which the strings point? What determines which way the tail of a comet points?

GUIDE FOR READING

◆ What are the characteristics of comets and asteroids?

◆ Where do meteoroids come from?

Reading Tip As you read, make an outline of this section using the headings as the main topics.

Imagine watching a cosmic collision! That's exactly what happened in July 1994. Eugene and Carolyn Shoemaker and David Levy discovered a new comet in 1993 that had previously broken into pieces near Jupiter. In 1994, the fragments returned and crashed into Jupiter. On Earth, astronomers were fascinated to see the huge explosions—some were as large as Earth!

As this story shows, the sun, planets, and moons aren't the only objects in the solar system. There are also millions of smaller objects, most of which are classified as comets and asteroids.

Comets

One of the most glorious things you can see in the night sky is a comet. A bright comet may be visible only for days or weeks or months, but is well worth seeing. In April 1997, for example, Comet Hale-Bopp and its bright dust tail were clearly visible even without a telescope.

You can think of a **comet** as a "dirty snowball" about the size of an Earth mountain. **Comets are chunks of ice and dust whose orbits are usually very long, narrow ellipses.** Because their orbits are so

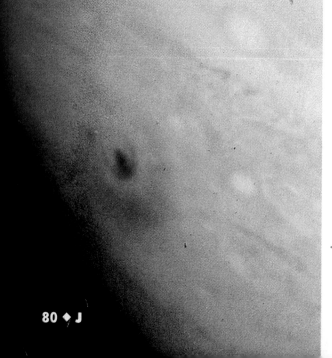

◀ A dark ring on Jupiter caused by comet Shoemaker-Levy 9

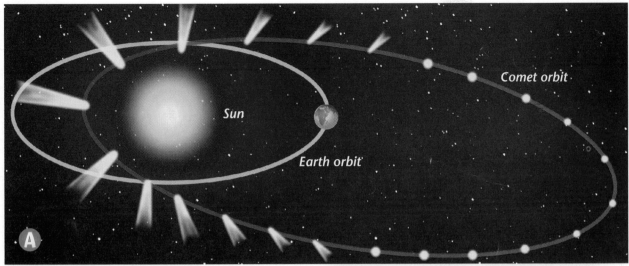

elliptical, few of them pass near Earth. They can usually then be seen only briefly. When a comet gets close enough to the sun, the energy in the sunlight turns the ice into gas, releasing dust. The gas and dust form an outer layer called the coma. Figure 28 shows the inner layer of the comet, which is then called the nucleus. The brightest part of a comet, the comet's head, is made up of the nucleus and coma.

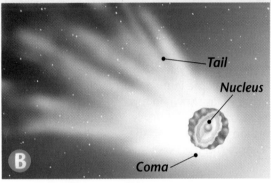

Figure 28 A. Most comets revolve around the sun in very long, narrow orbits. **B.** The main parts of a comet are the nucleus, the coma, and the tail. *Observing What shape is a comet's orbit?*

Remember that the sun's corona produces a stream of particles called the solar wind. Solar wind pushes the gas from a comet away from the sun. Gas and dust form the comet's tail. The tail looks like hair; in fact, the name *comet* means "long-haired star" in Greek.

A comet's tail can be hundreds of millions of kilometers long and stretch across most of the sky. The material is stretched out very thinly, however, so there isn't much mass in a comet tail.

In 1705, Edmond Halley, an English astronomer, calculated the orbits of 24 comets that people had observed over hundreds of years. Halley realized that several of the comets seemed to have the same orbit and suggested that they were actually the same comet. Halley calculated that this comet appeared about every 76 years, and predicted that it would reappear in 1758. When this prediction came true, the comet was named Halley's Comet. In 1986, the last time Halley's Comet appeared, the European Space Agency's *Giotto* spacecraft flew within a few hundred kilometers of it.

☑ *Checkpoint* How did Halley's Comet get its name?

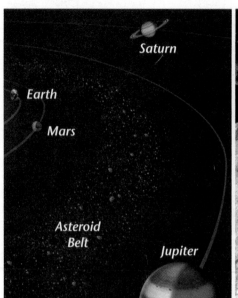

Figure 29 The asteroid belt (left) lies between Mars and Jupiter. Asteroids come in many sizes and shapes, as shown in this artist's depiction (center). NASA's *Galileo* mission photographed the asteroid Gaspra (right) .

Asteroids

Between 1801 and 1807, astronomers discovered four small objects between the orbits of Mars and Jupiter. They named the objects Ceres, Pallas, Juno, and Vesta. Over the next 80 years, astronomers found 300 more. These objects, called **asteroids,** are too small and too numerous to be considered full-fledged planets. **Most asteroids revolve around the sun between the orbits of Mars and Jupiter.** This region of the solar system, shown in Figure 29, is known as the **asteroid belt.**

Astronomers have discovered more than 10,000 asteroids, and more are found every month. Ceres, Pallas, Juno, and Vesta are among the dozen that are over 250 kilometers across.

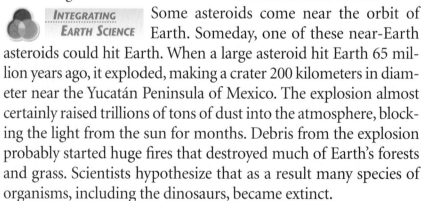 **INTEGRATING EARTH SCIENCE** Some asteroids come near the orbit of Earth. Someday, one of these near-Earth asteroids could hit Earth. When a large asteroid hit Earth 65 million years ago, it exploded, making a crater 200 kilometers in diameter near the Yucatán Peninsula of Mexico. The explosion almost certainly raised trillions of tons of dust into the atmosphere, blocking the light from the sun for months. Debris from the explosion probably started huge fires that destroyed much of Earth's forests and grass. Scientists hypothesize that as a result many species of organisms, including the dinosaurs, became extinct.

Meteors

Imagine being outside in the country on a clear night, looking up at the sky. Suddenly, you see a streak of light flashing across the sky. Within seconds, you see another streak. For an hour or so, you see a streak at least once a minute. You are watching a meteor shower. Meteor showers happen regularly, several times a year.

Even when there is no meteor shower, you frequently can see meteors if you are far from city lights and the sky is free of clouds. On average, a meteor streaks overhead every 10 minutes.

A **meteoroid** is a chunk of rock or dust in space. **Meteoroids usually come from comets or asteroids.** When a comet breaks up, it forms a cloud of dust that continues to move through the solar system. When Earth passes through one of these dust clouds, bits of dust enter Earth's atmosphere.

When a meteoroid enters Earth's atmosphere, friction makes it burn up and produce the streak of light you see in the sky—a **meteor.** If the meteoroid is large enough, it may not burn up completely. Meteoroids that pass through the atmosphere and hit Earth's surface are called **meteorites.** The craters on the moon and on other objects in the solar system were caused by meteoroids.

Meteorites fall all over Earth. Most of them look just like stones, so nobody notices them. A few meteorites are made almost entirely of iron and nickel, and so are unusually heavy for their size. This makes them more likely to be identified as meteorites than as Earth rocks.

Figure 30 A. Meteor Crater in Arizona is the best-known meteorite crater on Earth. It was formed when a meteorite hit Earth about 40,000 years ago. **B.** Meteoroids make streaks of light, like the one above, as they burn up in the atmosphere.

 Section 5 Review

1. What is a comet made of?
2. Where are most asteroids found?
3. What are the main sources of meteoroids?
4. What is the difference between a meteor and a meteorite?
5. **Thinking Critically** **Predicting** Describe what might happen if an asteroid the size of the one that hit Earth 65 million years ago hit Earth today.

Science at Home

Meteor showers occur regularly on specific dates. (The Perseids meteor shower, for example, occurs every August 12.) Look in the newspaper or almanac for information about the next meteor shower. With adult family members, go outside on that night and look for meteors. Explain to your family what causes the glow.

SECTION 6 Is There Life Beyond Earth?

DISCOVER ACTIVITY

Is Yeast Alive or Not?

1. Open a package of yeast and pour it into a bowl.
2. Look at the yeast carefully. Make a list of your observations.
3. Fill the bowl about halfway with warm water (about 20°C). Add a spoonful of sugar. Stir the mixture with the spoon. Wait five minutes.
4. Now look at the yeast again and make a list of your observations.

Think It Over

Forming Operational Definitions Which of your observations seem to suggest that yeast is not alive? Which observations suggest that yeast is alive? How can you tell if something is alive?

GUIDE FOR READING

- **What conditions do living things need to exist on Earth?**
- **Why do scientists think Mars and Europa are good places to look for signs of life?**

Reading Tip **As you read, write down evidence to support this statement: Life may exist in other parts of the solar system.**

Most of Antarctica is covered with snow and ice. You would not expect to see rocks lying on top of the whiteness. But surprisingly, in some places people have found rocks lying on the surface. When scientists examined the rocks, they found that the rocks are meteorites. A few of the meteorites came from Mars. Astronomers think that meteoroids hitting the surface of Mars must have blasted chunks of rock into space. The rocks eventually entered Earth's atmosphere and landed in Antarctica.

Recently a team of scientists announced that a meteorite from Mars found in Antarctica shows tiny shapes that look like fossils—the remains of ancient life preserved in rock. Many scientists doubt that the shapes really are fossils. But if they are, it would be a sign that life forms similar to bacteria once existed on Mars. Life other than that on Earth would be called **extraterrestrial life.**

Figure 31 Dr. Ursula Marvin (lying down) studies meteorites such as this one in Antarctica.

The "Goldilocks Conditions"

If you did the Discover activity, you saw that it can be hard to tell whether something is alive or not. But all living things on Earth have several characteristics in common. Living things are made up of one or more cells. Living things take in energy and use it to grow and develop. They reproduce, producing new living things of the same type. Living things also give off waste.

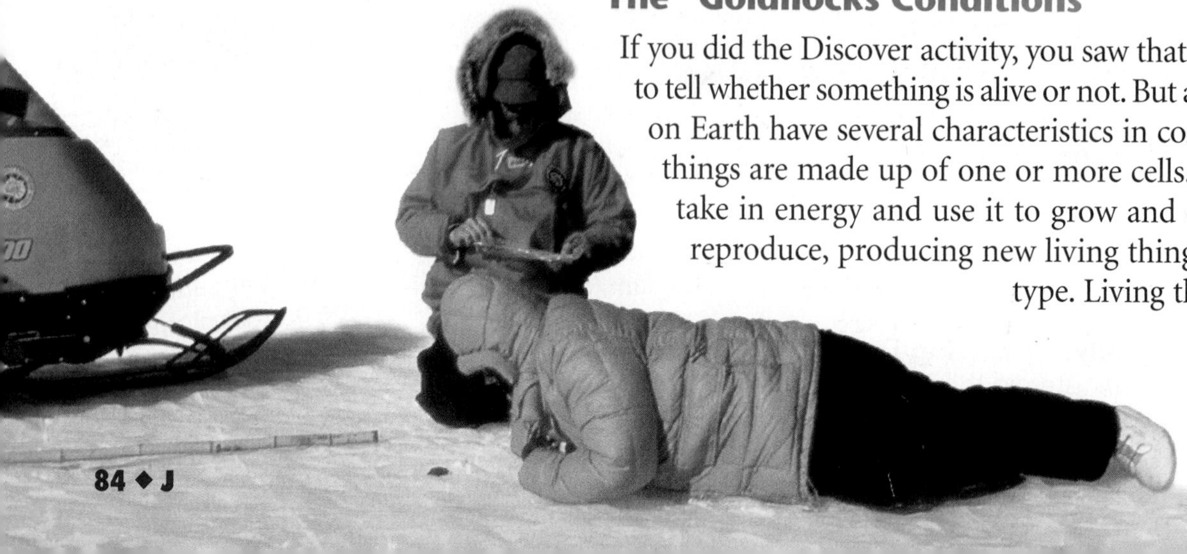

A yeast cell, for example, is a living thing. Each yeast organism has one cell. Yeast cells take in sugar for energy. They reproduce and make new yeast cells. And yeast cells produce carbon dioxide as waste. A yeast cell, then, fulfills all the requirements for a living thing.

Nobody knows whether life exists anywhere other than Earth. Scientists often talk about the conditions needed by "life as we know it." **Earth has liquid water and a suitable temperature range and atmosphere for living things to survive.** Other planets do not have such favorable conditions, which scientists sometimes call the "Goldilocks conditions." That is, the temperature is not too hot and not too cold. It is just right. If Earth were hotter, water would always be a gas—water vapor. If Earth were colder, water would always be solid ice. On Earth, water exists as a liquid as well as a solid and a gas.

Are these the conditions necessary for life? Or are they just the conditions that Earth's living things happen to need? Scientists have only one example of life to study: life on Earth. Unless scientists find life somewhere else, there will be no way to answer these questions.

✓ *Checkpoint* *What are some characteristics of all living things?*

Life on Earth

In recent years, astounding discoveries have been made deep under the ocean. Sunlight never penetrates there. But deep-diving submarines have discovered giant tube worms and other animals that live at very high pressure in the dark. Single-celled forms of life have been discovered that are different from plants, animals, or bacteria. These newly discovered life forms get their energy not from sunlight, but from chemicals. Other scientists have found tiny life forms in caves and deep inside solid rocks. Still other scientists have found life surviving in hot springs that had been thought to be too hot to support life.

The range of conditions in which life can exist is much greater than scientists once thought. Perhaps life forms exist that do not even need the "Goldilocks conditions"!

Communicating

You are writing a letter to a **ACTIVITY** friend who lives on another planet. Your friend has never been to Earth and has no idea what the planet is like. Explain in your letter why the conditions on Earth make it the ideal place for living things.

Figure 32 These colonies of microorganisms were discovered deep in a cave in Mexico. *Inferring How does studying unusual organisms like these help scientists predict what extraterrestrial life might be like?*

Life on Mars?

Recall that Mars is the planet most similar to Earth. That makes Mars the most obvious place to look for living things similar to those on Earth.

The *Viking* Missions In 1970, a spacecraft found regions on the surface of Mars that look like stream beds with criss-crossing paths of water. These shapes, shown in Figure 33, were almost certainly formed by flowing water. **Since life as we know it requires water, scientists hypothesize that Mars may have once had the conditions needed for life to exist.**

Twin *Viking* spacecraft reached Mars in 1976. Each had one part that landed on Mars's surface and another part that stayed in orbit, taking pictures of most of the surface. Each of the *Viking* landers carried a compact biology laboratory meant to search for life forms.

The biology laboratories on the landers tested the Martian air and soil for signs of life. Each laboratory was designed to see if there were life forms that used oxygen and gave off carbon dioxide, as many living things on Earth do. A robot scoop brought some soil from Mars's surface into the lab and added water to see if the sample gave off oxygen. None of these tests showed any evidence of life.

Checkpoint *What evidence shows that there may once have been running water on Mars?*

Meteorites From Mars Interest in life on Mars was increased by the report in 1996 about the meteorite from Mars that may contain fossils. The scientists' report started a huge debate. What were the tubelike things in the meteorite? Many scientists have suggested that the tiny shapes found in the meteorite do not prove that life forms once existed on Mars. Perhaps the shapes came from natural processes on Mars and are just lumps of hardened clay. Perhaps the shapes came from snow that got into cracks in the meteorite after it landed on Earth. Were the shapes

Figure 33 These patterns on the surface of Mars are probably evidence that liquid water once flowed on Mars. *Applying Concepts Why does this evidence make it more likely that there may once have been life on Mars?*

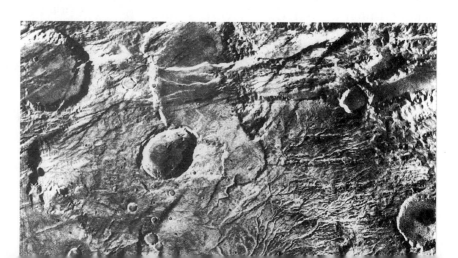

too deep inside the rocks to be from Earth? Perhaps the shapes are too small to be the remains of life forms. They are only one-hundredth the size of any other known life forms.

The most effective way to answer these questions is to send more probes to Mars. Future Mars missions should be able to bring samples of rocks and soil back to Earth for detailed analysis. Scientists may not yet have evidence of life on Mars, but hope is growing that we can soon solve the mystery.

Life on Europa?

Many scientists think that Europa, one of Jupiter's moons, may have the conditions necessary for life to develop. Photos from *Voyager* and *Galileo* showed that Europa has a very smooth, icy crust with giant cracks in it.

Close-up views from *Galileo* show that Europa's ice has broken up and re-formed, resulting in twisted, house-sized blocks of ice. Similar patterns occur in the ice crust over Earth's Arctic Ocean. Could this mean that there is a liquid ocean under Europa's ice? The water in the ocean could possibly be kept liquid by heat coming from inside Europa. **If there is liquid water on Europa, there might also be life.**

How can scientists study conditions under Europa's ice sheet? Such studies are many years off. People will have to wait for the next generation of space probes to search for liquid water on Europa.

Figure 34 Europa is covered with a layer of ice similar to the ice covering Earth's Arctic Ocean. There may be liquid water under the ice.

Section 6 Review

1. What conditions does life on Earth need to survive?
2. Why do astronomers think there could be life on Europa?
3. How did the *Viking* missions search for life on Mars?
4. **Thinking Critically** **Applying Concepts** Do you think there could be life as we know it on Venus? Explain. (*Hint:* Review page 66.)

Science at Home

Imagine that scientists have found intelligent extraterrestrial life. With family members, make up a message to send to the extraterrestrials. Remember that they will not understand English, so you should use only symbols and drawings in your message.

Space Exploration—Is It Worth the Cost?

Imagine that your spacecraft has just landed on Mars after a two-month journey from Earth. You've spent years planning for this moment. Canyons, craters, and distant plains stretch out before you. You check your spacesuit and prepare to step out onto the rocky red surface of Mars.

Is such a trip likely? Would it be worthwhile? How much is space flight really worth to human society? Scientists and politicians have already started to debate such questions. Space exploration can help us learn more about the universe. But exploration is risky and expensive. Sending people into space costs billions of dollars and risks human lives. How can we balance the costs and benefits of space exploration?

The Issues

Should Humans Travel Into Space? Many Americans think that Neil Armstrong's walk on the moon in 1969 was one of the great moments in history. Also, learning how to keep people alive in space has led to improvements in everyday life. Safer equipment for firefighters, easier ways to package frozen food, and effective heart monitors have all come out of space program research.

What Are the Alternatives? Space exploration can involve a project to put a person on Mars. It also can involve a more limited use of scientific instruments near Earth, such as the Hubble Space Telescope. Instead of sending people, we could send space probes like *Mars Pathfinder* to other planets.

Is Human Space Exploration Worth the Cost? Scientists who favor human travel into space say that only people can collect certain kinds of information. And using simpler space vehicles that are cheaper to build can also save money. But no one knows if research in space really provides information quicker than research that can be done on Earth. Many critics of space research think that other needs are more important. One United States senator said, "Every time you put money into the space station, there is a dime that won't be available for our children's education or for medical research."

You Decide

1. Identify the Problem
In your own words, list the costs and benefits of space exploration.

2. Analyze the Options
Make a chart of three different approaches to space exploration: sending humans to another planet, doing only Earth-based research, and one other option. What are the benefits and drawbacks of each approach?

3. Find a Solution
Imagine that you are a member of Congress who has to vote on a new budget. There is a fixed amount of money to spend, so you have to decide which needs are most important. Make a list of your top ten priorities. Explain your decisions.

SECTION 1 Observing the Solar System

Key Ideas

◆ Ptolemy thought that Earth is at the center of the system of planets.
◆ Copernicus thought that the sun is at the center of the planets. Galileo's observations supported Copernicus's theory.
◆ Kepler discovered that the orbits of the planets are ellipses.
◆ Newton concluded that two factors—inertia and gravity—combine to keep the planets in orbit.

Key Terms

geocentric   ellipse
heliocentric   inertia

 SECTION 2 The Sun

Key Ideas

◆ The sun's energy comes from nuclear fusion.
◆ The sun's atmosphere has three layers: the photosphere, the chromosphere, and the corona.
◆ Features on or above the sun's surface include sunspots, prominences, and solar flares.

Key Terms

nuclear fusion   solar wind
core   sunspot
photosphere   prominence
chromosphere   solar flare
corona

 SECTION 3 The Inner Planets

Key Idea

◆ The four inner planets—Mercury, Venus, Earth, and Mars—are small and have rocky surfaces. They are often called the terrestrial planets.

Key Terms

terrestrial planets
retrograde rotation
greenhouse effect

 SECTION 4 The Outer Planets

Key Ideas

◆ Four outer planets—Jupiter, Saturn, Uranus, and Neptune—are much larger than Earth.
◆ Pluto and Charon have solid surfaces and masses much less than that of Earth.

Key Term

gas giant

 SECTION 5 Comets, Asteroids, and Meteors

Key Ideas

◆ Comets are chunks of ice and dust that usually have long, elliptical orbits.
◆ Most asteroids revolve around the sun between the orbits of Mars and Jupiter.

Key Terms

comet   asteroid belt   meteor
asteroid   meteoroid   meteorite

SECTION 6 Is There Life Beyond Earth?

INTEGRATING LIFE SCIENCE

Key Ideas

◆ Earth has liquid water and a suitable temperature range and atmosphere for living things to survive.
◆ Since life as we know it requires water, scientists hypothesize that Mars may have once had the conditions for life to exist.

Key Term

extraterrestrial life

Organizing Information

Compare/Contrast Table On a separate piece of paper, make a table comparing and contrasting the geocentric and heliocentric systems. Include information on the following: object at the center of the system; objects that move around the center; who the system was first proposed by; and who supported the system. (For more on compare/contrast tables, see the Skills Handbook.)

Reviewing Content

For more review of key concepts, see the Interactive Student Tutorial CD-ROM.

Multiple Choice

Choose the letter of the answer that best completes each statement.

1. Copernicus thought that the solar system was
   a. celestial.
   b. elliptical.
   c. geocentric.
   d. heliocentric.

2. The part of the sun where nuclear fusion occurs is the
   a. photosphere.   b. chromosphere.
   c. corona.   d. core.

3. Planets with atmospheres composed mostly of carbon dioxide include
   a. Earth and Mercury.
   b. Venus and Mercury.
   c. Venus and Mars.
   d. Mercury and Mars.

4. The Great Red Spot is a huge storm on
   a. Jupiter.   b. Neptune.
   c. Saturn.   d. Pluto.

5. Most asteroids orbit the sun
   a. between the sun and Mercury.
   b. between Earth and Mars.
   c. between Mars and Jupiter.
   d. between Neptune and Pluto.

True or False

If the statement is true, write true. If it is false, change the underlined word or words to make the statement true.

6. The shape of the orbit of each planet is a <u>circle</u>.

7. Sunspots are regions of <u>cooler</u> gases on the sun.

8. The atmosphere of Venus has <u>higher</u> pressure than the atmosphere of Earth.

9. Aside from the sun, <u>Saturn</u> is the largest source of gravity in the solar system.

10. Conditions favorable to life as we know it are sometimes called the <u>Goldilocks conditions</u>.

Checking Concepts

11. How did Galileo's observations support the heliocentric system?

12. How did Newton's work on orbits add to the work Kepler had done?

13. Why is it usually impossible to see the sun's corona?

14. What are sunspots?

15. Why does Mercury have only a thin atmosphere?

16. How do astronomers explain that Venus rotates in the opposite direction from most planets and moons?

17. What are the major characteristics of the terrestrial planets? How do they differ from the gas giants?

18. Why do some astronomers think that Pluto should not be called a planet?

19. Why does a comet's tail always stream away from the sun?

20. Do living things have to live on the surface of a planet or moon? Where else on a planet or moon could scientists look for evidence of life?

21. **Writing to Learn** Imagine you are an astronaut on a mission to explore the solar system. Write a trip journal telling the story of your trip from Earth to another terrestrial planet and to a gas giant. Include a description of each planet.

Thinking Critically

22. **Relating Cause and Effect** How would Earth move if the sun (including its gravity) suddenly disappeared? Explain your answer.

23. **Applying Concepts** Explain why Venus is hotter than it would be without its atmosphere.

24. **Comparing and Contrasting** Compare and contrast meteoroids, meteors, and meteorites.

25. **Making Generalizations** Why would the discovery of liquid water on another planet be important?

Applying Skills

Use the diagram of an imaginary, newly discovered planetary system around Star X to answer Questions 26–28. The periods of revolution of planets A, B, and C are 75 Earth days, 200 Earth days, and 300 Earth days.

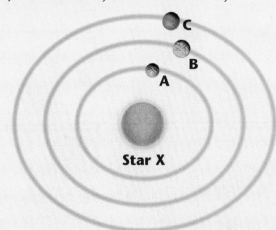

Star X

26. Interpreting Data Which planet in this new planetary system revolves around Star X in the shortest amount of time?

27. Making Models In 150 days, how far will each planet have revolved around Star X? Copy the diagram and sketch the positions of the three planets to find out. How far will each planet have revolved around Star X in 400 days? Sketch their positions.

28. Drawing Conclusions Can planet C ever be closer to planet A than to planet B? Study your drawings to figure this out.

Performance CHAPTER PROJECT 2 **Assessment**

Project Wrap Up Now you are ready to present your solar system. Explain how you were able to work with large distances. Display your data tables showing how you did the calculations and how you checked them for accuracy. Compare the distances in your models to distances inside and outside your classroom.

Reflect and Record In your journal, explain what you would change in your model of the solar system. What would you do to improve the model? How effectively did you use computers or calculators to get the data?

Test Preparation
Use these questions to prepare for standardized tests.

Study the table. Then answer Questions 29–32.

Planet	Period of Rotation (Earth days)	Period of Revolution (Earth years)	Average Distance From the Sun (million kilometers)
Mars	1.03	1.9	228
Jupiter	0.41	12	778
Saturn	0.43	29	1,427
Uranus	0.72	84	2,871
Neptune	0.67	165	4,497

29. Which of these planet's orbits is farthest from Earth's orbit?
 a. Mars   **b.** Jupiter
 c. Uranus   **d.** Neptune

30. Which planet has a "day" that is most similar in length to a day on Earth?
 a. Mars   **b.** Jupiter
 c. Uranus   **d.** Neptune

31. Light takes about 8 minutes and 20 seconds to travel from the sun to the Earth, 150 million kilometers away. About how long does it take light to travel from the sun to Jupiter?
 a. 10 minutes   **b.** 25 minutes
 c. 43 minutes   **d.** 112 minutes

32. Which one of the following conclusions about planets is supported by the information in the table?
 a. As distance from the sun increases, period of rotation increases.
 b. As distance from the sun increases, period of revolution increases.
 c. As distance from the sun increases, period of revolution decreases.
 d. There is no relationship between distance from the sun and period of revolution.

 CHAPTER

3 Stars, Galaxies, and the Universe

 WEB ACTIVITY www.phschool.com

Integrating Physics 🔵

PROJECT 3

Star Stories

In the spring of 1997, you could easily see comet Hale-Bopp, shown here, without any special equipment. But many of the objects astronomers study just look to you like tiny pinpoints of light—that is, if you can see them at all. However, astronomers have found many ways to learn about these "pinpoints."

In this chapter, you will discover how astronomers study the universe and what they have learned about the stars. In your project, you will find out how people in the past created stories to explain the patterns they saw in the sky. You'll learn how the names of constellations reflect the cultures of the people who named them.

Your Goal To recognize major constellations, learn the stories behind their names, and create your own star myth.

To complete the project you will
◆ learn the star patterns of at least three major constellations
◆ research the myths that gave one constellation its name
◆ write a new star myth

Get Started Begin your project by previewing page 94 to learn what a constellation is. With a group of your classmates, make a list of constellations you have heard about. Then look at the star charts in Appendix B. From the chart for the current season, choose three or four constellations to explore further.

Check Your Progress You'll be working on this project as you study this chapter. To keep your project on track, look for Check Your Progress boxes at the following points.

Section 1 Review, page 100: Locate constellations and research one.
Section 3 Review, page 116: Draw a new picture for the star pattern in your constellation and give it a name.
Section 5 Review, page 124: Write a story about your constellation.

Wrap Up At the end of the chapter (page 127), you will present your constellation along with a story that explains its name.

These telescopes on top of Mauna Kea, a mountain in Hawaii, are used to study distant stars and galaxies.

 SECTION 4 Star Systems and Galaxies

Discover Why Does the Milky Way Look Hazy?
Try This A Spiral Galaxy

 SECTION 5 History of the Universe

Discover How Does the Universe Expand?

SECTION 1 Tools of Modern Astronomy

DISCOVER ·· ACTIVITY····

Are Those Stars Really a Group?

1. Cut ten pieces of thread to different lengths between 5 cm and 25 cm. Tape a 1-cm plastic foam ball to the end of each piece of thread.

2. Obtain a piece of cardboard about 50 cm by 50 cm. Tape the free ends of the thread pieces to various points on the cardboard.

3. Turn the cardboard over so the balls hang down. While your partner holds the cardboard horizontally, look at the balls from the side.

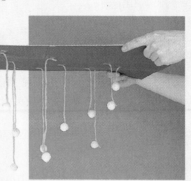

4. Imagine that the balls are stars in a constellation. With one eye closed, sketch the pattern the balls make.

Think It Over

Observing Can you tell which balls are farther away and which are closer? Do you think you can tell how close to each other the stars in a constellation are?

GUIDE FOR READING

◆ What is the electromagnetic spectrum?

◆ What is the main purpose of a telescope?

◆ Why do astronomers use spectrographs?

Reading Tip Before you read, rewrite the main headings of the section as *how, why,* or *what* questions.

Before the Civil War, thousands of enslaved African Americans fled north to freedom. Traveling in secret by night, they looked to the stars for direction. They told each other to "follow the drinking gourd"—the star pattern that points to the North Star. Most Americans today call this pattern the Big Dipper.

Patterns of stars in the sky are called **constellations.** Stars in a constellation can look as if they are close together, even though they are at very different distances from Earth. For example, the star at the end of the handle in the Big Dipper is about twice as far from Earth as most of the other stars in the Big Dipper. So the stars in a constellation are not, in fact, all close together. Constellations are just patterns formed by stars that happen to be in the same direction in the sky.

Big Dipper ▶

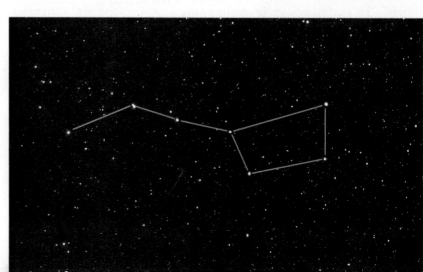

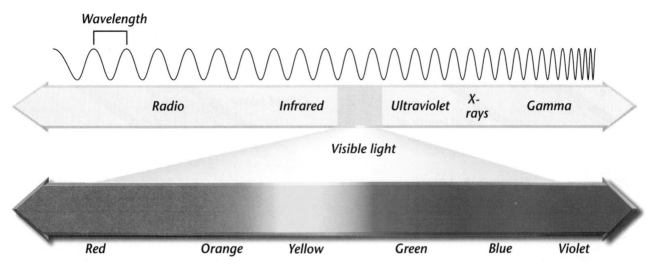

Wavelength

Radio Infrared Ultraviolet X-rays Gamma

Visible light

Red Orange Yellow Green Blue Violet

Figure 1 The electromagnetic spectrum ranges from long-wavelength radio waves through short-wavelength gamma rays. *Interpreting Diagrams Are infrared waves longer or shorter than ultraviolet waves?*

Electromagnetic Radiation

The stars in constellations appear as tiny points of light. In fact, stars are huge spheres of hot glowing gas, like the sun. By using telescopes to study the light from stars, astronomers have learned a great deal about stars and other objects in the sky.

Types of Electromagnetic Radiation Scientists call the light you see with your eyes **visible light.** Light is a form of **electromagnetic radiation** (ih lek troh mag NET ik), or energy that can travel directly through space in the form of waves.

Visible light is only one type of electromagnetic radiation. Many objects give off radiation that you can't see. For example, the glowing coils of an electric heater give off infrared radiation, which you feel as heat. Radio waves carry signals to radios and televisions.

The Electromagnetic Spectrum As you can see in Figure 1, the distance between the crest of one wave and the crest of the next wave is called the **wavelength.** Visible light has very short wavelengths, less than one millionth of a meter. Some electromagnetic waves have even shorter wavelengths. Other waves are much longer, even several meters long.

If you shine white light through a prism, the light spreads out to make a range of different colors with different wavelengths, called a **spectrum.** The spectrum of visible light is composed of the colors red, orange, yellow, green, blue, and violet. **The electromagnetic spectrum includes radio waves, infrared radiation, visible light, ultraviolet radiation, X-rays, and gamma rays.** All these different kinds of electromagnetic waves make up the electromagnetic spectrum, shown in Figure 1.

Checkpoint Give two examples of electromagnetic waves that you might use or experience every day.

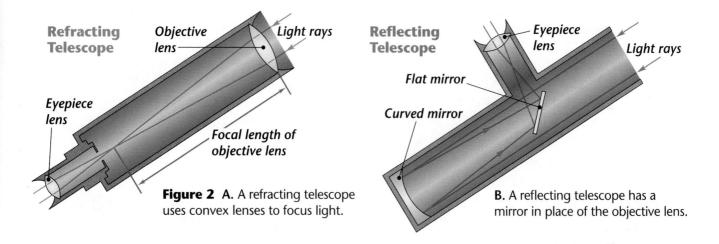

Refracting Telescope — Objective lens — Light rays — Eyepiece lens — Focal length of objective lens

Reflecting Telescope — Eyepiece lens — Light rays — Flat mirror — Curved mirror

Figure 2 A. A refracting telescope uses convex lenses to focus light.

B. A reflecting telescope has a mirror in place of the objective lens.

Locating Radio Waves

You can use an umbrella to focus radio waves.

ACTIVITY

1. Line the inside of an umbrella with aluminum foil.

2. Turn on a small radio and tune it to a station.

3. Move the radio up and down along the umbrella handle. Find the position where the station is clearest. Radio waves reflecting off the foil focus at this point. Tape the radio to the handle.

4. Hold the umbrella at different angles. At which angle is the station the clearest?

Inferring In which direction do you think the radio station is located? Explain.

Telescopes

Objects in space give off all types of electromagnetic radiation. Many telescopes produce images using visible light. But much of modern astronomy is based on detection of other types of electromagnetic radiation. **Most telescopes collect and focus different types of electromagnetic radiation, including visible light.**

Visible Light Telescopes In 1609, Galileo used a refracting telescope to look at objects in the sky. A **refracting telescope** uses convex lenses to gather a large amount of light and focus it onto a small area. A **convex lens** is a piece of transparent glass, curved so that the middle is thicker than the edges.

Galileo's telescope, like the refracting telescope in Figure 2, used two lenses—an eyepiece lens and an objective lens. When light passes through the objective lens, the lens focuses the light at a certain distance away from the lens. This distance is called the focal length of the lens. Different lenses have different focal lengths. The larger the objective lens, the more light it can collect, making it easier for astronomers to see faint objects.

Isaac Newton built the first **reflecting telescope** in 1668. It used a mirror instead of an objective lens. Like the lenses in a refracting telescope, the mirror in a reflecting telescope focuses a large amount of light onto a small area. The larger the mirror, the more light the telescope can collect. The largest visible light telescopes are now all reflecting telescopes.

Radio Telescopes Devices used to detect radio waves from objects in space are called **radio telescopes.** Most radio telescopes have curved, reflecting surfaces—up to 305 meters in diameter. These surfaces focus radio waves the way the mirror in a reflecting telescope focuses light waves. The surfaces of radio telescopes concentrate the faint radio waves from outer space onto small antennas like those on radios. As with visible light telescopes, the larger a radio telescope is, the more radio waves it can collect.

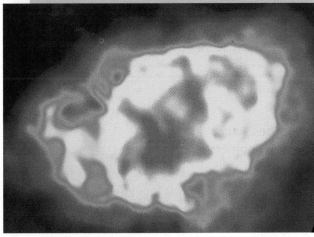

Figure 3 The Crab Nebula is the remains of a star that exploded about 1,000 years ago. The top image was photographed using visible light. The lower image was made using radio waves.

Other Telescopes Some telescopes detect infrared radiation, which has longer wavelengths than visible light. There are also telescopes that detect the shortest wavelengths—ultraviolet radiation, X-rays, and gamma rays.

✓ *Checkpoint* *What are two types of visible light telescopes?*

Observatories

A building that contains one or more telescopes is called an **observatory.** Most large observatories are located on mountaintops. Why have astronomers built the largest visible light telescopes on the tops of mountains? Earth's atmosphere makes objects in space look blurry. The sky on some mountaintops is clearer and is not brightened much by city lights.

The best observatory site on Earth is probably the top of Mauna Kea, an ancient volcano on the island of Hawaii. Mauna Kea is so tall—4,200 meters above sea level—that it is above 40 percent of Earth's atmosphere. The sky there is very dark at night, and many nights are free of clouds.

To collect data from visible light telescopes on Earth, astronomers must stay awake all night. Radio telescopes, however, can be used 24 hours a day and do not have to be on mountaintops.

Satellites

 INTEGRATING TECHNOLOGY Most ultraviolet radiation, X-rays, and gamma rays are blocked by Earth's atmosphere. To detect these wavelengths, astronomers have placed telescopes on satellites.

The Hubble Space Telescope is a reflecting telescope with a mirror 2.4 meters in diameter. Because it is above the atmosphere, it makes images in visible light that are about seven times more detailed than the best images from telescopes on Earth. The Hubble Space Telescope can also collect ultraviolet and infrared radiation. The Chandra X-ray Observatory, similar in size to Hubble, makes images in the X-ray portion of the spectrum.

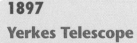 **SCIENCE & History**

Development of Modern Telescopes

During the last century, astronomers have built larger telescopes, which can collect more light and other types of radiation. Today's astronomers use tools that could not have been imagined 100 years ago.

1897

Yerkes Telescope

The 1-meter-diameter telescope at Yerkes Observatory in Wisconsin is the largest refracting telescope ever built. Because its main lens is so large, the Yerkes telescope can collect more light than any other refracting telescope.

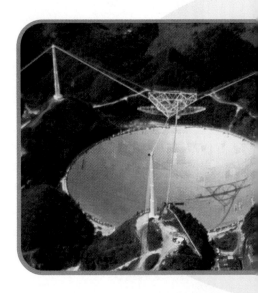

1900   **1920**   **1940**

1931

Beginning of Radio Astronomy

Karl Jansky, an American engineer, was trying to find the source of static that was interfering with radio communications. Using a large antenna, he discovered that the static was coming from objects in space giving off radio waves. Jansky's accidental discovery led to the beginning of radio astronomy.

Spectrographs

Most large telescopes today have spectrographs. A **spectrograph** (SPEK truh graf) breaks the light from an object into colors and photographs the resulting spectrum. **Astronomers use spectrographs to get information about stars, including their chemical compositions and temperatures.**

Chemical Compositions Chemical elements in a star's atmosphere absorb light from the star. Each element absorbs light at different wavelengths, and each absorbed wavelength is shown as a dark line on a spectrum. Just as each person has a unique set of fingerprints, each element has a unique set of lines. By comparing

In Your Journal

Research one of these telescopes or another large telescope. Create a publicity brochure in which you describe the telescope's features, when and where it was built, and what types of research it is used for.

1963
Arecibo Radio Telescope

This radio telescope in Puerto Rico was built in a natural bowl in the ground. It is 305 meters in diameter, more than three times the size of the next-largest radio telescope.

1990
Hubble Space Telescope

The Hubble Space Telescope can see objects in space more clearly than any other telescope. Astronauts have visited the telescope several times to repair or replace equipment.

1960	1980	2000

1980
Very Large Array

The Very Large Array is a set of 27 radio telescopes in New Mexico. The telescopes can be moved close together or far apart. The telescopes are linked, so they can be used as if they were one giant telescope 25 kilometers in diameter.

1999
Chandra X-ray Observatory

The hottest objects in space give off X-rays. NASA launched the Chandra X-ray Observatory into orbit to make detailed images in that part of the spectrum. Chandra X-ray images match Hubble visible-light images in detail.

Figure 4 Astronomers can use line spectrums to find the temperatures of stars.

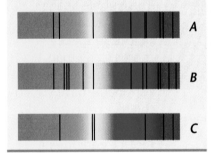
a star's spectrum with the known spectrums of different elements, such as those shown in Figure 4, astronomers can infer which elements are found in a star.

Temperatures Most stars have a chemical composition similar to the sun, about 73% hydrogen, 25% helium, and 2% other elements. The amount of energy each of these elements absorbs depends on the temperature of the star. Because of this, stars at different temperatures produce different line spectrums. By comparing a star's spectrum with the known spectrums of elements at different temperatures, astronomers can infer how hot the star is. Hydrogen, for example, produces very strong spectral lines when it is at about 10,000 degrees Celsius. If astronomers do not see a strong hydrogen line on a spectrum, this does not mean there is no hydrogen in the star. It just means that the star is much cooler or hotter than 10,000 degrees Celsius.

Section 1 Review

1. What are the main types of electromagnetic waves, from longest wavelength to shortest?
2. For what purpose are most telescopes designed?
3. What can astronomers tell from looking at a star's spectrum?
4. How are the stars in a constellation related to each other in space?
5. **Thinking Critically** **Applying Concepts** Why are images from the Hubble Space Telescope clearer than images from telescopes on Earth?

Check Your Progress

CHAPTER PROJECT 3

Using the star charts in Appendix B, try to locate constellations in the night sky. (*Hint:* Remember that you may be looking at a constellation upside down. Also, light conditions may affect how many stars you can see.) Sketch the constellations you can locate and compare them with the ones your classmates saw. Now choose one constellation and research the myths or legends that gave it its name. Find as many stories as you can about your constellation and make notes about them.

Make Your Own Telescope

In this lab you will learn how to construct and use a simple refracting telescope. You can then try out your telescope.

Problem

How can you build a telescope?

Skill Focus

making models, observing, drawing conclusions

Materials

2 paper towel tubes of slightly different
   diameters
plastic objective lens
plastic eyepiece lens
foam holder for eyepiece (optional)
transparent tape
meter stick

Procedure

1. Fit one of the paper towel tubes inside the other. Make sure you can move the tubes but that they will not slide on their own.

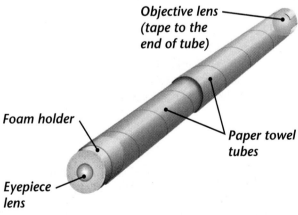

Objective lens
(tape to the
end of tube)

Paper towel
tubes

Foam holder

Eyepiece
lens

2. Place the large objective lens flat against the end of the outer tube. Tape the lens in place.

3. Insert the small eyepiece lens into the opening in the foam holder.
4. Place the foam eyepiece lens holder into the inner tube at the end of the telescope opposite to the objective lens.
5. Tape a meter stick to the wall. Look through the eyepiece at the meter stick from 5 m away. Slide the tubes in and out to focus your telescope so that you can clearly read the numbers on the meter stick. Draw your telescope. On the drawing, mark the tube position that allows you to read the numbers most clearly.
6. Use your telescope to look at other objects at different distances, both in your classroom and through the window. For each object you view, draw your telescope, marking the tube position at which you see the object most clearly. **CAUTION:** *Do not look at the sun. You will damage your eyes.*

Analyze and Conclude

1. Why do you need two tubes?
2. If you focus on a nearby object and then focus on something farther away, do you have to move the tubes together or apart?
3. How does this telescope compare to the telescopes astronomers use?
4. **Apply** How could you improve on the design of your telescope? What effects would different lenses or tubes have?

More to Explore

With an adult, go outside in the evening a few days after the first-quarter phase and observe the moon. Draw a circle with all the features you see. Label the maria (lowlands) and highlands.

Light Pollution

Imagine you are in a dark theater watching a movie when the lights come on. You can still see the movie, but it seems dull and faded. For the same reason, you may not see very many stars if you live in or near a city. Light from street lights and advertising signs masks much of the starlight. Artificial light that makes it difficult to see the night sky clearly is known as light pollution.

Astronomers build modern observatories far from cities and outdoor lights. But light pollution is still a problem for older observatories and for amateur astronomers like the one in this photo. If light pollution increases, how will you see glittering stars in the night sky, the broad Milky Way, meteor showers, or an occasional passing comet?

The Issues

How Important Are Outdoor Lights?
Artificial lighting is one of the great advantages of the modern age. Street lights make it easier to drive safely, reducing accidents. Night lighting allows businesses to stay open later. In addition, lighting helps people feel safer in their homes and on the streets.

What Can Be Done? Street lights are the biggest cause of light pollution. However, some types of street lights cause more light pollution than others. The three types of street light bulbs are mercury vapor bulbs, high-pressure sodium bulbs, and low-pressure sodium bulbs. Low-pressure sodium lights cause the least problem for astronomers because they shine in only a very narrow range of wavelengths. A simple filter on a telescope can eliminate this light from the telescope's view. In addition, street lights of all types can be shielded so they don't shine upward. They can also be pointed only where the light is needed.

Would Reducing Light Pollution Save Money? Mercury vapor lights are the most common type of street light. High-pressure sodium and low-pressure sodium lights use less electricity, however.

Modifying street lights to reduce light pollution would initially cost a lot of money. However, reducing unneeded light and using light bulbs that require less electricity would also reduce energy usage, which could save money.

You Decide

1. Identify the Problem
In your own words, explain the problem of light pollution.

2. Analyze the Options
List possible solutions. What procedures are involved in each solution? List the advantages and disadvantages of each solution.

3. Find a Solution
Find out what types of street lights your town or city has. Are the lights shielded? Write a letter to your city council proposing a solution to light pollution in your city or town.

SECTION 2 Characteristics of Stars

DISCOVER •• ACTIVITY ••••

How Does Your Thumb Move?

1. Stand facing a wall, at least an arm's length away. Stretch your arm out with your thumb up and your fingers curled.

2. Close your right eye and look at your thumb with your left eye. Line your thumb up with something on the wall.

3. Now close your left eye and open your right eye. How does your thumb appear to move along the wall?

4. Bring your thumb closer to your eye, about half the distance as before. Repeat Steps 2 and 3.

Think It Over

Observing How does your thumb appear to move in Step 4 compared to Step 3? How are these observations related to how far away your thumb is at each step? How could you use this method to estimate distances?

Imagine you could travel to the stars at the speed of light. To travel from Earth to the sun would take about 8 minutes, not very long for such a long trip! Yet the next nearest star, Proxima Centauri, is much farther away—a trip to Proxima Centauri would take 4.2 years!

Most stars are much farther away than Proxima Centauri. Our sun and Proxima Centauri are only two of the stars that make up the Milky Way. The Milky Way is a giant flat structure, called a **galaxy,** that contains hundreds of billions of stars. At the speed of light, it would take you 25,000 years to travel the 250 million billion kilometers to the center of our galaxy. If you left our galaxy and traveled at the speed of light for about 2 million years, you would eventually reach another galaxy, the Andromeda Galaxy.

There are billions of galaxies in the **universe,** which astronomers define as all of space and everything in it. Since galaxies are so far apart, most of the universe is empty space. If our galaxy were the size of a dime, the Andromeda Galaxy would be about half a meter away. The rest of the universe, as far as astronomers can see, would extend for about 2 kilometers in all directions.

GUIDE FOR READING

◆ How do astronomers measure distances to nearby stars?

◆ How are stars classified?

Reading Tip As you read, make a list of the characteristics of stars. Write a sentence describing each characteristic.

Distances to Stars

Distances on Earth are often measured in kilometers. However, as you have seen, distances to stars are so large that the kilometer is not a very practical unit. Instead of kilometers, astronomers use a unit called the light-year. In space, light travels at a speed of 300,000 kilometers per second. A **light-year** is the distance that light travels in one year, or about 9.5 million million kilometers. Note that the light-year is a unit of distance, not time.

To help you understand what a light-year is, consider an everyday example. If you bicycle at 10 kilometers per hour, it would take you 1 hour to go to a mall 10 kilometers away. You could say that the mall is "1 bicycle-hour" away.

It takes light about 4.2 years to reach Earth from Proxima Centauri, so Proxima Centauri is 4.2 light-years, or 40 million million kilometers, away.

✓ *Checkpoint* *How many kilometers are in three light-years?*

Measuring Distances to Stars

Standing on Earth looking up at the sky, it seems as if there is no way to tell how far away the stars are. However, astronomers have found a way to measure those distances. **Astronomers often use parallax to measure distances to nearby stars.**

Parallax is the apparent change in position of an object when you look at it from different places. For example, imagine that you and a friend have gone to a movie. After you sit down, a woman with a large hat sits down in front of you. Because you and your friend are sitting in different positions, the woman's hat blocks different parts of the screen. If you are sitting on her left, the woman's hat appears to be in front of the dinosaur. But to your friend, who is sitting on her right, she appears to be in front of the bird.

Have the woman and her hat moved? No. But because of your relative positions, she appears to have moved. This apparent movement is parallax.

Astronomers use parallax to measure the distances to nearby stars. They look at a star when Earth is on one side of the sun. Then they

Figure 5 You and your friend are sitting behind a woman with a large hat.
Applying Concepts Why is your view of the screen different from your friend's view?

Your view

Your friend's view

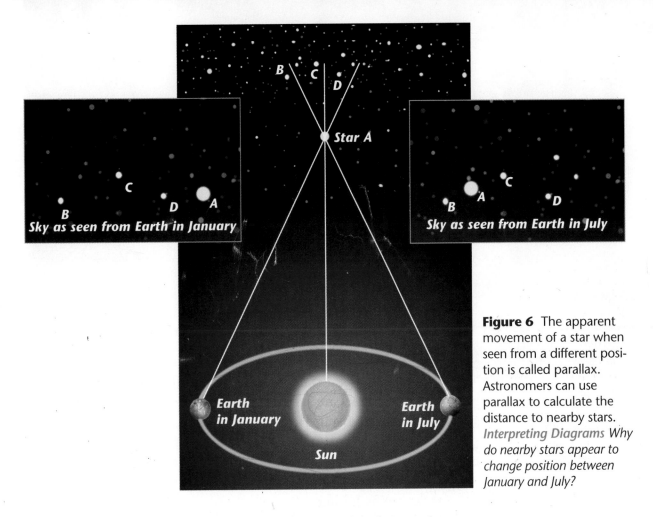

Star A

C
B
D **A**

Sky as seen from Earth in January

B **C**
D

C
B **A** **D**

Sky as seen from Earth in July

Earth in January

Sun

Earth in July

Figure 6 The apparent movement of a star when seen from a different position is called parallax. Astronomers can use parallax to calculate the distance to nearby stars. *Interpreting Diagrams* Why do nearby stars appear to change position between January and July?

look at the same star again six months later, when Earth is on the other side of the sun. Astronomers measure how much the star appears to move against a background of stars that are much farther away. They can then use this measurement, called the parallax shift, to calculate how far away the star is. The less the star appears to move, the farther away it is.

Parallax cannot be used to measure distances any greater than 1,000 light-years using existing technology. The distance that a star that far away would appear to move when seen from opposite sides of Earth's orbit is too small to measure accurately.

Classifying Stars

Like the sun, all stars are huge spheres of glowing gas. They are made up mostly of hydrogen, and they make energy by nuclear fusion. This energy makes stars shine brightly. The sun is only an average-brightness star. However, the sun is much closer to Earth than any other star. Because it is so close, the sun appears much brighter and much larger then any other star. But the sun is neither the brightest nor the largest star in the galaxy.

Astronomers classify stars according to their physical characteristics. **The main characteristics used to classify stars are size, temperature, and brightness.**

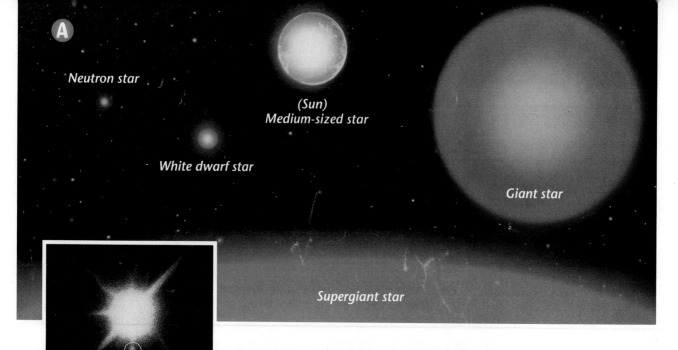

A

Neutron star

(Sun)
Medium-sized star

White dwarf star

Giant star

B

Supergiant star

Figure 7 A. Stars range in size from tiny neutron stars to enormous supergiants. B. The brighter star is Sirius A. The fainter star circled in yellow, Sirius B, is a white dwarf. *Observing What size star is the sun?*

Sizes of Stars

When you look at stars in the sky, they all appear to be the same size. Many stars are actually about the size of the sun, which is a medium-sized star. However, some stars are much larger than the sun. Very large stars are called **giant stars** or supergiant stars. If the supergiant star Betelgeuse (BAY tul jooz) were located where our sun is, it would be large enough to fill the solar system as far out as Jupiter.

Some stars are much smaller than the sun. White dwarf stars are about the size of Earth. Neutron stars are even smaller, only about 20 kilometers in diameter.

✓ *Checkpoint Name five sizes of stars, in order from largest to smallest.*

Color and Temperature of Stars

If you look around the sky at night, you can see slight differences in the colors of the stars. Figure 8 shows the constellation known as Orion the Hunter. The red star in Orion's shoulder is Betelgeuse. The blue-white star in Orion's heel is called Rigel.

A star's color reveals its temperature. Hot objects on Earth display the same range of colors as stars. If you watch a toaster heat up, you can see the wires glow red-hot. The wires inside a light bulb are even hotter and glow white. Similarly, the coolest stars—about 3,200 degrees Celsius—appear reddish in the sky. Reddish Betelgeuse is a cool star. With a surface temperature of about 5,500 degrees Celsius, the sun glows white. The hottest stars in the sky—over 10,000 degrees Celsius—appear slightly bluer than the sun. Blue-white Rigel is a very hot star, more than 15,000 degrees Celsius.

Brightness of Stars

Stars also differ in brightness, the amount of light they give off. The brightness of a star depends upon its size and temperature. Recall from Chapter 2 that the photosphere is the layer of a star that gives off light. Betelgeuse is fairly cool, so each square meter of its photosphere doesn't give off much light. But Betelgeuse is very large, so it shines brightly. Rigel, on the other hand, is very hot, so each square meter of Rigel's photosphere gives off a lot of light. Even though it is much smaller than Betelgeuse, Rigel also shines brightly.

How bright a star looks from Earth depends on both how far the star is from Earth and how bright the star actually is. Because of these two factors, the brightness of a star can be described in two different ways: apparent magnitude and absolute magnitude.

Apparent Magnitude A star's **apparent magnitude** is its brightness as seen from Earth. Astronomers can measure apparent magnitude fairly easily using electronic devices.

Astronomers cannot tell how much light a star gives off just from the star's apparent magnitude. Just as a flashlight looks brighter the closer it is to you, a star looks brighter the closer it is to Earth. For example, the sun looks very bright. This does not mean that the sun gives off more light than all other stars. The sun looks so bright simply because it is so close to Earth.

Social Studies
CONNECTION

During the Middle Ages Arab astronomers in Southwest Asia and North Africa named many stars. For example, the star name Algol comes from the Arabic words *Ras al Ghul*, which mean "the demon's head." Other Arabic star names include Aldebaran ("the follower of the Pleiades"), Vega ("swooping eagle"), and Rigel ("the left leg of the giant").

In Your Journal

Many other words used in astronomy and mathematics come from Arabic. Find *zenith*, *nadir*, *algorithm*, and *algebra* in a dictionary. Write their definitions in your own words.

Figure 8 The constellation Orion includes the red supergiant star Betelgeuse and the blue supergiant star Rigel.

Figure 9 The stars in a globular cluster are all about the same distance from Earth.

Star Bright ACTIVITY

Here's how you can compare absolute and apparent magnitudes.

1. Dim the lights. Put two equally bright flashlights next to each other on a table. Turn them on.

2. Look at the flashlights from the other side of the room. Think of the flashlights as two stars. Then compare them in terms of absolute and apparent magnitudes.

3. Move one of the flashlights closer to you and repeat Step 2.

4. Replace one of the flashlights with a brighter one. Repeat Step 1 with the unequally bright flashlights. Then repeat Step 2.

Making Models How could you place the flashlights in Step 4 so that they have the same apparent magnitude? Try it.

Absolute Magnitude   A star's **absolute magnitude** is the brightness the star would have if it were at a standard distance from Earth. Finding a star's absolute magnitude is more complicated than finding its apparent magnitude. An astronomer must first find out the star's apparent magnitude and its distance from Earth. The astronomer can then calculate the star's brightness if it were at a standard distance from Earth.

Figure 9 shows a globular cluster, a group of 10,000 to 1,000,000 stars that are close together. The stars in a globular cluster are all at about the same distance from Earth. So astronomers study globular clusters to compare the brightnesses of stars. If one star in a globular cluster appears brighter than another star, it really is brighter than that other star.

The Hertzsprung-Russell Diagram

Two of the most important characteristics of stars are temperature and absolute magnitude. About 100 years ago, Ejnar Hertzsprung (EYE nahr HURT sprung) in Denmark and Henry Norris Russell in the United States each made graphs to find out if temperature and brightness are related. They plotted the temperatures of stars on the x-axis and their brightness on the y-axis. The points formed a pattern.

The graph they made is still used by astronomers. It is called the **Hertzsprung-Russell diagram,** or H-R diagram. As you can see in Figure 10, most of the stars in the H-R diagram form a diagonal line called the **main sequence.** In the main sequence, surface temperature increases as brightness increases. More than 90% of all stars are main-sequence stars. The sun is among the stars on the main sequence. Giant and supergiant stars are higher and farther to the right on the H-R diagram. White dwarfs are hot, but not very bright, so they appear at the bottom center of the diagram.

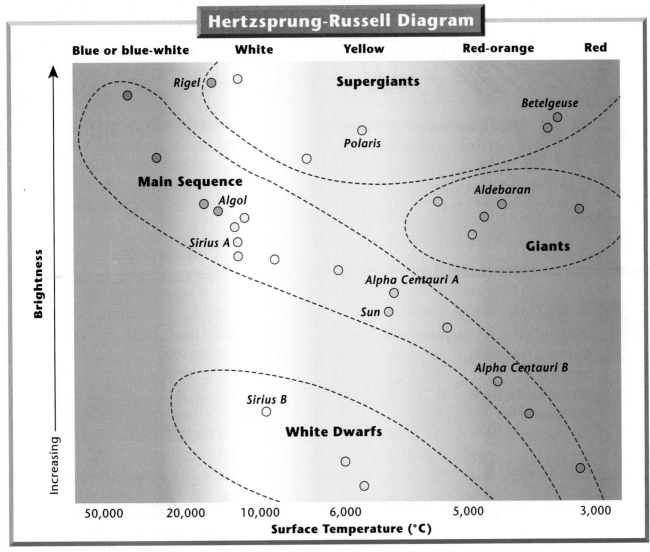

Hertzsprung-Russell Diagram

Blue or blue-white   White   Yellow   Red-orange   Red

Rigel

Supergiants

Betelgeuse

Polaris

Main Sequence

Algol

Aldebaran

Sirius A

Giants

Alpha Centauri A

Sun

Alpha Centauri B

Sirius B

White Dwarfs

Brightness

Increasing

Surface Temperature (°C)

50,000   20,000   10,000   6,000   5,000   3,000

Figure 10 The Hertzsprung-Russell diagram shows the
relationship between surface temperature and brightness.
Interpreting Diagrams Which star is hotter: Rigel or Aldebaran?

Section 2 Review

1. What is parallax? How is it useful in astronomy?
2. List three characteristics used to classify stars.
3. Which is hotter—a red star or a blue star? Why?
4. **Thinking Critically Applying Concepts** Stars A and B
   have about the same apparent magnitude, but Star A is about
   twice as far from Earth as Star B. Which star has the greater
   absolute magnitude? Explain your answer.

Science at Home

With adult family members,
go outside on a clear, dark
night. Determine which way
is north, south, east, and west.
Using the star chart for the
correct season in Appendix B,
look for the constellation Orion.
Find the stars Betelgeuse and
Rigel in Orion and explain to
your family why they are
different colors.

HOW FAR IS THAT STAR?

When astronomers measure parallax, they record the positions of stars on film in cameras attached to telescopes. In this lab, you will set up a model of a telescope and use it to estimate distances.

Problem

How can parallax be used to determine distances?

Materials

masking tape   paper clips   pen
black and red pencils metric ruler   paper
meter stick   calculator
lamp without a shade, with 100-watt light bulb
copier paper box (without the lid)
flat rectangular table, about 1 m wide

Procedure

Part 1 Telescope Model

1. Place the lamp on a table in the middle of the classroom.
2. Carefully use the tip of the pen to make a small hole in the middle of one end of the box. The box represents a telescope.
3. At the front of the classroom, place the box on a flat table so the hole points toward the lamp. Line the left side of the box up with the left edge of the table.

4. Put a small piece of tape on the table below the hole. Use the pen to make a mark on the tape directly below the hole. The mark represents the position of the telescope when Earth is on one side of its orbit.

Part 2 Star 1

5. Label a sheet of paper Star 1 and place it inside the box as shown in the drawing. Hold the paper in place with two paper clips. The paper represents the film in a telescope.
6. Darken the room. Turn on the light to represent the star.
7. With the red pencil, mark the paper where you see a dot of light. Label this dot A. Dot A represents the image of the star on the film.
8. Move the box so the right edge of the box lines up with the right edge of the table. Repeat Step 4. The mark on the tape represents the position of the telescope six months later, when Earth is on the other side of its orbit.
9. Repeat Step 7, and use a black pencil to mark the second dot B. Dot B represents the image of the star as seen 6 months later from the other side of Earth's orbit.
10. Remove the paper. Before you continue, copy the data table into your notebook.
11. Measure and record the distance in millimeters between dots A and B. This distance represents the parallax shift for Star 1.

DATA TABLE

Star	Parallax Shift (mm)	Focal Length (mm)	Diameter of Orbit (mm)	Calculated Distance to Star (mm)	Calculated Distance to Star (m)	Actual Distance to Star (m)

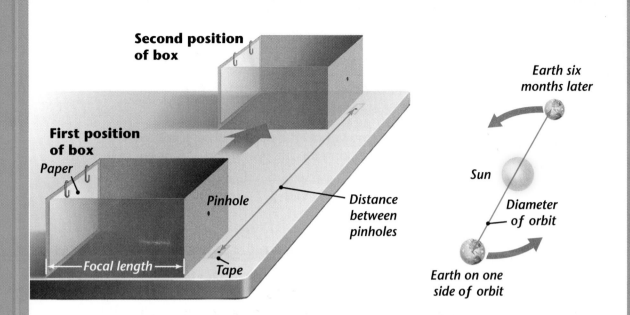

Second position of box

First position of box

Paper

Pinhole

Focal length

Tape

Distance between pinholes

Earth six months later

Sun

Diameter of orbit

Earth on one side of orbit

12. Measure and record the distance from the hole in the box to the lamp. This distance represents the actual distance to the star.

13. Measure and record the distance from the hole (lens) to the back of the box in millimeters. This distance represents the focal length of your telescope.

14. Measure and record the distance in millimeters between the marks on the two pieces of masking tape. This distance represents the diameter of Earth's orbit.

Part 3 Stars 2 and 3

15. Move the lamp away from the table—about half the distance to the back of the room. The bulb now represents Star 2. Predict what you think will happen to the light images on your paper.

16. Repeat Steps 6–12 with a new sheet of paper to find the parallax shift for Star 2.

17. Move the lamp to the back of the classroom. The bulb now represents Star 3. Repeat Steps 6–12 with a new sheet of paper to find the parallax shift for Star 3.

Analyze and Conclude

1. What caused the apparent change in position of the dots of light for each star? Explain.

2. Use the following formula to calculate the distance from the telescope to Star 1.

$$\text{Distance} = \frac{\text{Diameter} \times \text{Focal length}}{\text{Parallax shift}}$$

3. Divide your result from Question 3 by 1,000 to get the distance to the light bulb in meters.

4. Repeat Questions 3 and 4 for Stars 2 and 3.

5. Was your prediction in Step 15 correct? Why or why not?

6. Is the parallax shift greater or smaller the farther away the star is? Relate each star's parallax shift to its distance from Earth.

7. **Think About It** How did your calculation for Star 3 compare with the actual distance? What could you do to improve your results?

Design an Experiment

What would happen if you kept moving the lamp away from the box? Is there a distance at which you can no longer find the distance to the star? Design an experiment to find out.

SECTION
3 Lives of Stars

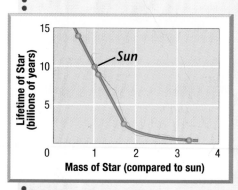

What Determines How Long Stars Live?

1. This graph shows how the mass of a star is related to its lifetime—how long the star lives before it runs out of fuel.

2. How long does a star with 0.8 times the mass of the sun live? How long does a star with 1.7 times the mass of the sun live?

Think It Over

Drawing Conclusions Describe the general relationship between a star's mass and its lifetime.

GUIDE FOR READING

◆ How does the life of a star begin?

◆ What determines how long a star will live?

◆ What happens to a star when it runs out of fuel?

Reading Tip As you read, make a flowchart showing the stages in the life of a medium-sized star.

Jocelyn Bell today ▼

In 1967, Jocelyn Bell, a British astronomy student, detected an object in space that appeared to give off regular pulses of radio waves. Some astronomers hypothesized that the pulses might be a signal from an extraterrestrial civilization. At first, astronomers even named the source LGM, for the "Little Green Men" in early science-fiction stories. Eventually, astronomers concluded that the source of the radio waves was a neutron star. A neutron star is a tiny star left over when a giant star explodes. Neutron stars like the one Bell discovered are called **pulsars**, short for pulsating radio sources.

Studying the Lives of Stars

Stars do not last forever. Each star is born, goes through its life cycle, and eventually dies. (Of course, stars are not really alive. The words *born, live,* and *die* are just helpful comparisons.) How did astronomers figure out that the neutron star Bell discovered had been a larger star earlier in its life?

Imagine that you want to study how people age. You wish you could watch a few people for 50 years, but your assignment is due next week! You have to study a lot of people for a short time, and classify the people into different age groups. You may come up with groups like *babies, children, teenagers, young adults, middle-aged people,* and *elderly people.* You don't have time to see a single person go through all these stages, but you know the stages exist.

Astronomers have a similar problem with stars. They can't watch a single star for billions of years, so they study many stars and see how they differ from one another.

A Star Is Born

A star is made up of a large amount of gas in a relatively small volume. A **nebula,** on the other hand, is a large amount of gas and dust spread out in an immense volume. All stars begin their lives as parts of nebulas.

Gravity can pull some of the gas and dust in a nebula together. The contracting cloud is then called a protostar. *Proto* means "earliest" in Greek, so a **protostar** is the earliest stage of a star's life. **A star is born when the contracting gas and dust become so hot that nuclear fusion starts.** Recall from Chapter 2 that nuclear fusion is the process by which atoms of hydrogen are combined to form helium. During fusion, enormous amounts of energy are released.

Lifetimes of Stars

Before they can tell how old a star is, astronomers must determine its mass. **How long a star lives depends on how much mass it has.**

You might think that stars with more mass would last longer than stars with less mass. However, the reverse is true. You can think of stars as being like cars. A small car has a small gas tank, but it also has a small engine that burns gas slowly. A large car, on the other hand, has a larger gas tank, but it also has a larger engine that burns gas rapidly. So the small car might be able to travel farther on one small tank of gas than the larger car can on one large tank of gas. Small-mass stars use up their fuel more slowly than large-mass stars, so they have much longer lives.

Generally, stars that have less mass than the sun use their fuel slowly, and can live for up to 200 billion years. Medium-mass stars like the sun live for about 10 billion years. Astronomers think the sun is about 4.6 billion years old, so it is almost halfway through its lifetime.

Stars that have more mass than the sun have shorter lifetimes. A star that is 15 times as massive as the sun may live only about ten million years. That may seem like a long time, but it is only one tenth of one percent of the lifetime of the sun.

✓ *Checkpoint* *If a star is twice as massive as the sun, will it have a longer or shorter life than the sun?*

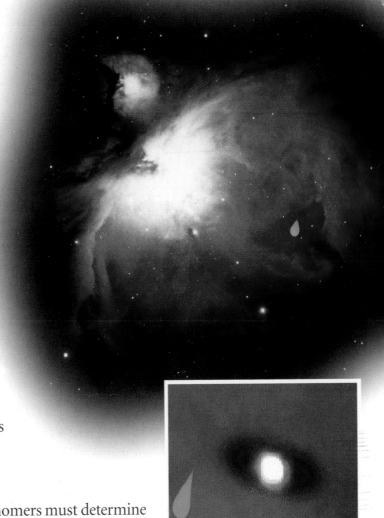

Figure 11 The Orion Nebula, top, is a giant cloud of gas and dust. The Hubble Space Telescope took this photo of a protostar, bottom, in the Orion Nebula. A protostar is a star in the earliest stage of its life. *Applying Concepts How do some of the gas and dust in a nebula become a protostar?*

Figure 12 Supernova 1987A was the brightest supernova seen in hundreds of years. The arrow in the photo at the left points to the original star, before it exploded. *Making Generalizations Why were ancient astronomers able to see supernovas?*

Predicting ACTIVITY

Find Algol, Polaris, and Sirius B in the H-R diagram on page 109. For each star, write a sentence predicting what the next stages in its life will be.

Deaths of Stars

When a star begins to run out of fuel, the center of the star shrinks and the outer part of the star expands. The star becomes a red giant or supergiant.

All main sequence stars eventually become red giants or supergiants. However, what happens next depends on the mass of the star, as *Exploring the Lives of Stars* shows. **When a star runs out of fuel, it becomes a white dwarf, a neutron star, or a black hole.**

White Dwarfs Small- and medium-mass stars take 10 billion or more years to use up their nuclear fuel. Then their outer layers expand, and they become red giants. Eventually, the outer parts grow bigger still and drift out into space. The blue-white hot core of the star that is left behind is a **white dwarf.**

White dwarfs are only about the size of Earth, but they have about as much mass as the sun. Since a white dwarf has the same mass as the sun but only one millionth the volume, it is one million times as dense as the sun. A spoonful of material from a white dwarf has as much mass as a large truck. White dwarfs have no fuel, but they glow faintly from leftover energy. When a white dwarf stops glowing, it is dead. Then it is called a black dwarf.

Neutron Stars A dying giant or supergiant star can suddenly explode. Within hours, the star blazes millions of times brighter. The explosion is called a **supernova.** You can see a supernova in Figure 12. After a supernova, some of the material from the star expands into space. This material may become part of a nebula. The nebula can then contract to form a new, "recycled" star. Astronomers think the sun began as a nebula that contained material from a supernova explosion.

After the star explodes, some of the material from the star is left behind. This material forms a neutron star. **Neutron stars** are even smaller and denser than white dwarfs. A neutron star may contain as much as three times the mass of the sun but be only about 20 kilometers in diameter, the size of a large asteroid or a town on Earth.

Black Holes The most massive stars—those having more than 40 times the mass of the sun—become **black holes** when they die. After this kind of star becomes a supernova, more than five times the mass of the sun may be left. The gravity of this mass is so strong that the gas is pulled inward, packing the gas into a smaller and smaller space. Eventually five times as much mass as the sun becomes packed within a sphere 30 kilometers in diameter. At that point, the gravity is so strong that nothing can escape, not even light. The remains of the star become a black hole.

EXPLORING the Lives of Stars

A star's life history depends on its mass. The sun is a medium-mass star that will become a white dwarf, then a black dwarf.

Red Giant or Supergiant

When a star begins to run out of fuel, it expands to become a giant or supergiant.

A star's life begins when gas and dust in a nebula contract to form a protostar.

Protostar

Nebula

Giant and supergiant stars can blow up into supernovas.

Small and medium stars become red giants and then white dwarfs.

Supernova

White Dwarf

The remains of the most massive stars collapse into black holes. Not even light can escape from a black hole.

When a white dwarf runs out of energy, it turns into a black dwarf.

Black Hole

The remains of the supernova become a neutron star.

Neutron Star

Black Dwarf

Figure 13 This artist's impression shows a black hole pulling matter from a companion star. The material glows as it is pulled into the black hole. *Applying Concepts If it is impossible to detect a black hole directly, how do astronomers find them?*

No light, radio waves, or any other form of radiation can ever get out of a black hole, so it is not possible to detect a black hole directly. But astronomers can detect black holes indirectly.

For example, gas near a black hole is pulled so strongly that it rotates faster and faster around the black hole. Friction heats the gas up. Astronomers can detect X-rays coming from the hot gas and infer that a black hole is present. Similarly, if another star is near a black hole, astronomers can calculate the mass of the black hole from the effect of its gravity on the star. Scientists are using the Chandra X-ray Observatory to look for black holes by studying sources of X-rays.

Quasars In the 1960s, astronomers discovered objects that are unusual because they are very bright, but also very far away. Many of these objects are about 12 billion light-years away, making them among the most distant objects in the universe. These distant bright objects looked almost like stars. Since *quasi* means "something like" in Latin, these objects were given the name quasi-stellar objects, or **quasars.**

What could be so bright even though it is so far away? Astronomers have concluded that quasars are actually distant galaxies with giant black holes at their centers. Each black hole has a mass a billion times or more as great as that of the sun. As enormous amounts of gas revolve around such a black hole, the gas heats up and shines brightly.

Section 3 Review

1. What is the earliest stage in the life of a star?
2. Why do small-mass stars have longer lifetimes than large-mass stars?
3. What is the difference between stars that become white dwarfs and stars that become neutron stars?
4. What evidence do astronomers use to detect black holes?
5. **Thinking Critically Inferring** What will happen to the sun when it dies? Explain your answer.

Check Your Progress

CHAPTER PROJECT 3

Draw and label the stars in your constellation *without* the connecting lines that form the usual image. What different patterns can you see? (*Hint:* Use a pencil to "doodle" different connections among the stars.) What does each pattern look like? Choose one pattern, and use it to name your constellation. Then write an outline of a brief story that explains why this constellation is in the sky.

SECTION 4 Star Systems and Galaxies

DISCOVER .... ACTIVITY....

Why Does the Milky Way Look Hazy?

1. Using a pencil, carefully poke at least 20 holes close together in a sheet of white paper.

2. Tape the paper to a chalkboard or dark-colored wall.

3. Go to the other side of the room and look at the paper. From the far side of the room, what do the dots look like? Can you see individual dots?

Think It Over

Making Models How is looking at the paper from the far side of the room like trying to see many very distant stars that are close together? How does your model compare to the photograph of the Milky Way below?

On a clear, dark summer night in the country, you can see a hazy band of light stretched across the sky. This band of stars is called the Milky Way. It looks as if the Milky Way is very far away from Earth. Actually, though, Earth is inside the Milky Way! How is this possible? Before you can understand the answer to this question, you need to know more about how stars are grouped together.

Star Systems and Planets

Our solar system has only one star, the sun. **But more than half of all stars are members of groups of two or more stars, called star systems.** If you were on a planet in one of these star systems, you would probably see two or more suns in the sky.

Double and Triple Stars Star systems with two stars are called double stars or **binary stars.** (The prefix *bi* means "two.") Those with three stars are called triple stars. Proxima Centauri is probably part of a triple star system close to our sun. The other two stars in the system, Alpha Centauri A and Alpha Centauri B, form a double star. Scientists are not sure whether Proxima Centauri is really part of the system or is just passing close to the other two stars temporarily.

Astronomers can sometimes detect a binary star even if only one of the stars in the pair can be seen from Earth. For example, the darker star in the pair may pass in front of the other star and eclipse the other star. A system in which one star blocks the light from another is

GUIDE FOR READING

◆ What is a star system?
◆ What are the three types of galaxies?

Reading Tip Before you read, preview the boldfaced terms. As you read, look for a photograph or diagram that illustrates each term.

The Milky Way ▶

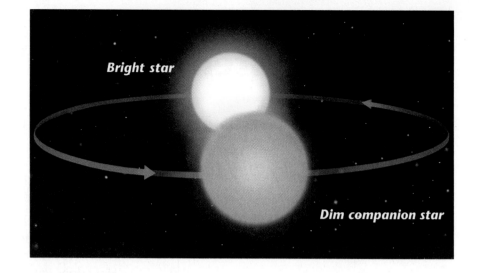

Figure 14 Algol is an eclipsing binary star system consisting of a bright star and a dim companion. Each time the dimmer star passes in front of the brighter one, Algol appears less bright.
Interpreting Diagrams When does Algol appear brighter?

Bright star

Dim companion star

Figure 15 If you saw someone dancing but couldn't see a partner, you could infer that the partner was there by watching the dancer you could see. Astronomers use a similar method to detect faint stars in star systems.

called an **eclipsing binary.** As Figure 14 shows, the star Algol is actually an eclipsing binary.

Often astronomers can tell that there is a second star in a system only by observing the effects of its gravity. As the second star revolves around the first star, the second star's gravity makes the first star move back and forth. Imagine you are watching a pair of dancers twirling each other around. Even if one dancer were invisible, you could tell that the invisible dancer was there from watching the motion of the visible dancer.

Planets Around Other Stars In 1995, astronomers discovered a planet revolving around a star using a method similar to the one they use to detect binary stars. The star the astronomers were observing, 51 Pegasi, moved back and forth only very slightly. Therefore, they knew the invisible object could not have enough mass to be a star. They deduced that it must be a planet.

Before this discovery, there was no way to know whether stars other than the sun had planets revolving around them. Now astronomers know that our solar system is not the only one. Most of the planets found beyond our solar system so far are very large, at least half Jupiter's mass. A small planet would be difficult to detect because it would have little gravitational effect on the star it revolved around.

Astronomers are trying to find new ways to use telescopes to see planets directly. Seeing a planet around another star is like trying to see a firefly near a street light. The glare of the light makes it hard to see anything near the light. To see a planet directly, astronomers will have to shield their view from the glare of the star that the planet revolves around. In 2000, astronomers were excited by the discovery of a planet orbiting a star similar to our sun and only 10.5 light-years away.

 INTEGRATING LIFE SCIENCE Some scientists hypothesize that life may exist on planets revolving around other stars. A few astronomers are using radio telescopes to search for signals that could not have come from natural sources. Such a signal might be evidence that an extraterrestrial civilization existed and was sending out radio waves.

☑ Checkpoint *What evidence have astronomers used to conclude that there are planets around other stars?*

Galaxies

Now you are ready to learn about the Milky Way. The Milky Way is the galaxy in which our solar system is located. Like other galaxies, it contains single stars, double stars, star systems, and lots of gas and dust between the stars. The Milky Way Galaxy, often just called "our galaxy," looks milky or hazy because the stars are too close together for your eyes to see them individually. The dark blotches in the Milky Way are clouds of dust that block light coming from stars behind them.

There are billions of galaxies in the universe. **Astronomers have classified most galaxies into three main categories: spiral galaxies, elliptical galaxies, and irregular galaxies.**

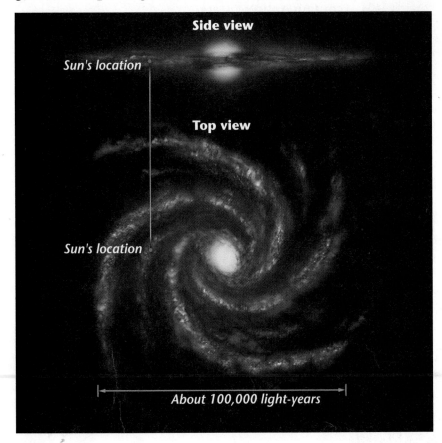

Side view

Sun's location

Top view

Sun's location

About 100,000 light-years

A Spiral Galaxy

You can make a model of our galaxy.

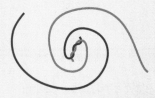

1. Using pipe cleaners, make a pinwheel with two spirals.

2. View the spirals along the surface of the table. Sketch what you see. Can you see the spiral shape?

3. Next, view the spirals from above the table and sketch them.

Observing The sun is inside a flat spiral galaxy. From Earth's position on the flat surface, is it possible to get a good view of stars in the spiral arms? Why or why not?

Figure 16 From the side, the Milky Way Galaxy appears to be a narrow disk. The spiral structure would be visible only from above the galaxy.

Figure 17 **A.** This spiral galaxy is similar to our galaxy. **B.** An elliptical galaxy looks like a flattened ball. **C.** The Large Magellanic Cloud is an irregular galaxy.

Spiral Galaxies Figure 17A shows a galaxy that has the shape of twin spirals, called a **spiral galaxy.** Astronomers can see other spiral galaxies from different angles. These views show that spiral galaxies have arms that spiral outward, like pinwheels.

Our galaxy has the same spiral, pinwheel shape. It is hard for us to see the spiral shape of our galaxy because our solar system is inside the galaxy, about two thirds of the way out in one of the spiral arms. The Milky Way you see in the sky is the view people on Earth get when they look toward the main part of the rest of our galaxy. The center of our galaxy is about 25,000 light-years from the sun. However, we cannot see the center of our galaxy. The center is hidden from our view by the dust associated with the massive clouds of gas between the sun and the center.

Elliptical Galaxies Not all galaxies have spiral arms. **Elliptical galaxies** look like flattened balls. These galaxies contain billions of stars but have little gas and dust between the stars. Because of the lack of gas and dust, new stars cannot form in most elliptical galaxies. Most elliptical galaxies contain only old stars.

Irregular Galaxies Some galaxies do not have regular shapes. Because of this, they are known as **irregular galaxies.** The Large Magellanic Cloud is an irregular galaxy about 160,000 light-years away from our galaxy. At this distance it is one of the closest neighboring galaxies in the universe.

Section 4 Review

1. What is a star system?
2. Describe the three main types of galaxies.
3. Where is the sun in our galaxy?
4. **Thinking Critically** **Applying Concepts** Some binary stars are called eclipsing binaries. Explain why this term is appropriate. (*Hint:* Think about Algol as you come up with an answer.)

Science at Home

Plan an evening of stargazing with adult family members. Choose a dark, clear night. Use binoculars if available and the star charts in Appendix B to locate the Milky Way and some interesting stars you have learned about. Explain to your family what you know about the Milky Way and each star you observe.

SECTION 5 History of the Universe

DISCOVER  ACTIVITY

How Does the Universe Expand?

1. Use a marker to put 10 dots on an empty balloon. The dots represent galaxies.
2. Blow up the balloon. What happens to the distances between galaxies that are close together? Galaxies that are far apart?

Think It Over

Inferring If the universe is expanding, do galaxies that are close together move apart faster or slower than galaxies that are far apart?

The Andromeda Galaxy is the most distant object you can see with your unaided eyes. Light from this galaxy has traveled for 2 million years before reaching your eyes. When that light finally reaches your eye, you are seeing what the galaxy looked like 2 million years ago. It is as though you are looking back in time.

Astronomers have photographed galaxies that are billions of light-years away. Light from these galaxies traveled for billions of years before it reached telescopes on Earth. From these observations, astronomers have inferred that the universe is incredibly old—billions of years old.

GUIDE FOR READING

◆ How did the universe form?
◆ How did the solar system form?

Reading Tip Before you read, write down what you have already heard about the big bang theory. Then read how the theory explains the history of the universe.

Moving Galaxies

To study how and when the universe formed, astronomers use information about how galaxies are moving. Astronomers can measure how far away different galaxies are. By examining the spectrum of a galaxy, astronomers can tell how fast the galaxy is moving and whether it is moving toward our galaxy or away from it. Only a few nearby galaxies are moving toward our galaxy. All of the other galaxies are moving away from our galaxy.

In the 1920s, Edwin Hubble, an American astronomer, discovered that the farther away a galaxy is from us, the faster it is moving away from us. The Hubble Space Telescope was named after Hubble in honor of this and other important discoveries.

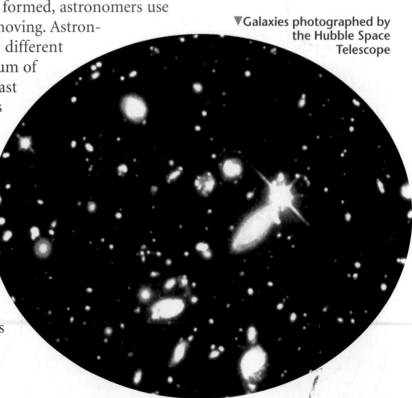

▼ Galaxies photographed by the Hubble Space Telescope

Figure 18 The galaxies in the expanding universe are like the raisins in rising bread dough. *Making Models How does rising raisin bread dough model the expanding universe?*

To understand how the galaxies are moving, think of raisin bread dough that is rising. If you could shrink yourself to sit on a raisin, you would see all the other raisins moving away from you as the bread dough rose. The farther away a raisin was from you, the faster it would move away, because there would be more bread dough to expand between you and the raisin. No matter which raisin you sat on, all the other raisins would seem to be moving away from you. You could tell that the bread dough was expanding by watching the other raisins.

The universe is like the raisin bread dough. The galaxies in the universe, like the raisins in the dough, are moving away from each other. In the universe it is space that is expanding, like the dough between the raisins.

The Big Bang Theory

To understand how the galaxies moved in the past, imagine you could run time backward. All of the galaxies would then be moving together instead of apart. All of the matter in the universe would eventually come together at a single point. At that time, billions of years ago, the universe was small, hot, and dense. The universe then exploded in what astronomers call the **big bang.**

According to the big bang theory, the universe formed in an enormous explosion about 10 to 15 billion years ago. Since the big bang, the universe has been expanding rapidly. Because of the big bang, the universe is billions of times larger than it was billions of years ago. To understand this change in size, picture a

Figure 19 All of the distant galaxies astronomers have observed are moving away from our galaxy.

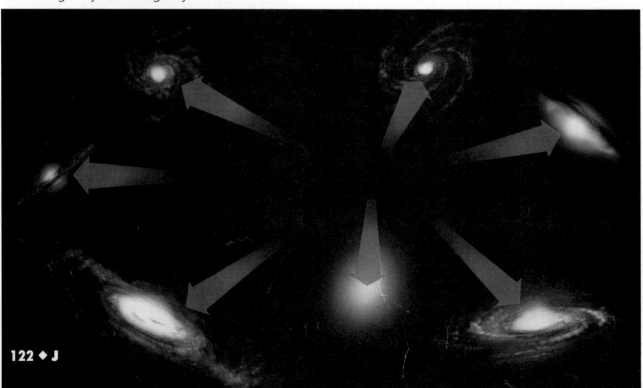

Figure 20 The solar system formed from a collapsing cloud of gas and dust.

Images (within figure):
- A cloud of gas and dust formed a spinning disk.
- Gas in the center of the disk collapsed to form the sun.
- The remaining gas and dust formed the planets.
- The solar system includes the sun, planets, and belts of rock, ice, and dust.

tiny pea. Pretend you can blow it up to be as big as Earth. You would be inflating the pea by about a billion times. Like the pea, the universe in which you live was once very small. The universe has been growing rapidly ever since the big bang. Astronomers have concluded that the galaxies are moving away from each other as a result of the big bang.

Since astronomers know approximately how fast the universe is expanding now, they can infer how long it has been expanding. Astronomers estimate that the universe has been expanding for 10 billion to 15 billion years.

☑ *Checkpoint* *Which way are most galaxies moving relative to each other?*

Formation of the Solar System

After the big bang, matter in the universe separated into galaxies. Gas and dust spread throughout space in our galaxy. Where the solar system is now, there was only cold, dark gas and dust.

About five billion years ago, a giant cloud of gas and dust, or nebula, collapsed to form the solar system. Slowly the nebula shrank to form a spinning disk. As gravity pulled some of the gas into the center of the disk, the gas became hot and dense enough for nuclear fusion to begin. The sun was born.

Elsewhere in the disk, gas and dust formed solid spheres smaller than the sun. The spheres closest to the sun lost most of their gases and became the inner planets Mercury, Venus, Earth, and Mars. The spheres farthest from the sun became the gas giants Jupiter, Saturn, Uranus, and Neptune. Between the inner planets and the gas giants, the asteroids formed. Beyond the gas giants, a huge cloud of ice and other substances formed. This cloud is probably the main source of comets. Pluto also formed in this region.

Figure 21 This engineer is checking data from the Hubble Space Telescope. The telescope can be controlled from this room.

The Future of the Universe

What will happen to the universe in the future? One possibility is that the universe will continue to expand, as it is doing now. All of the stars will eventually run out of fuel and burn out, and the universe will be cold and dark. Another possibility is that the force of gravity will begin to pull the galaxies back together. The result will be a reverse big bang, or "big crunch." All of the matter in the universe will be crushed into an enormous black hole.

Which of these possibilities is more likely? The answer depends on how strong the total force of gravity pulling the galaxies together is. This force depends on the total mass of the universe. It is very difficult for astronomers to estimate this mass because much of it is in the form of particles that do not give off electromagnetic radiation. The evidence so far suggests that the total mass of the universe is not great enough to pull the galaxies back together again. However, more research needs to be done to solve this problem.

Astronomy is one of the oldest sciences, but there are still many discoveries to be made and puzzles to be solved about this universe of ours!

Section 5 Review

1. What was the big bang?
2. Describe how the solar system formed.
3. What observations show that the universe is expanding?
4. **Thinking Critically Inferring** What can astronomers infer from the fact that other galaxies are moving away from ours?

Check Your Progress

CHAPTER PROJECT
3

Now you are ready to write the first draft of a story that explains your constellation's name. After you have written a first draft, read it over carefully and look for ways to improve it. Here are things to look for as you edit your first draft. Does the beginning grab the reader's interest? Does your story make sense? Should you add more details? Should you rethink your choice of words? Rewrite and revise as much as necessary.

SECTION 1 — Tools of Modern Astronomy

INTEGRATING PHYSICS

Key Ideas

◆ The electromagnetic spectrum includes radio waves, infrared radiation, visible light, ultraviolet radiation, X-rays, and gamma rays.

◆ Telescopes collect and focus different types of electromagnetic radiation.

◆ Astronomers use spectrographs to get information about stars.

Key Terms

constellation	refracting telescope
visible light	convex lens
electromagnetic	reflecting telescope
radiation	radio telescope
wavelength	observatory
spectrum	spectrograph

SECTION 2 — Characteristics of Stars

Key Ideas

◆ Astronomers use parallax to measure distances to nearby stars.

◆ The main characteristics used to classify stars are size, temperature, and brightness.

Key Terms

galaxy	apparent magnitude
universe	absolute magnitude
light-year	Hertzsprung-Russell diagram
parallax	main sequence
giant star	

SECTION 3 — Lives of Stars

Key Ideas

◆ A star is born when nuclear fusion starts.

◆ The length of a star's life depends on its mass.

◆ When a star runs out of fuel, it becomes a white dwarf, a neutron star, or a black hole.

Key Terms

pulsar	white dwarf	black hole
nebula	supernova	quasar
protostar	neutron star	

SECTION 4 — Star Systems and Galaxies

Key Ideas

◆ More than half of all stars are members of groups of two or more stars, called star systems.

◆ There are three types of galaxies: spiral galaxies, elliptical galaxies, and irregular galaxies.

Key Terms

binary star	elliptical galaxy
eclipsing binary	irregular galaxy
spiral galaxy	

SECTION 5 — History of the Universe

Key Ideas

◆ According to the big bang theory, the universe formed in an enormous explosion about 10 to 15 billion years ago.

◆ About five billion years ago, a cloud of gas and dust collapsed to form the solar system.

Key Term

big bang

Organizing Information

Concept Map Copy the concept map about telescopes onto a separate sheet of paper. Then complete it and add a title. (For more on concept maps, see the Skills Handbook.)

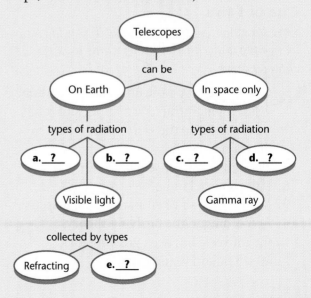

Reviewing Content

 For more review of key concepts, see the Interactive Student Tutorial CD-ROM.

Multiple Choice

Choose the letter of the answer that best completes each statement.

1. The Hubble Space Telescope is a
   a. gamma ray telescope.
   b. reflecting telescope.
   c. refracting telescope.
   d. radio telescope.
2. The most common chemical element in a star is
   a. hydrogen.
   b. helium.
   c. carbon.
   d. sodium.
3. To measure the distance to a nearby star, an astronomer would use
   a. visible light.
   b. quasars.
   c. parallax.
   d. a spectrograph.
4. Stars more massive than the sun
   a. live longer than the sun.
   b. are redder than the sun.
   c. have shorter lives than the sun.
   d. live as long as the sun.
5. The sun formed out of a
   a. pulsar.   b. supergiant star.
   c. black hole.   d. nebula.

True or False

If the statement is true, write true. If it is false, change the underlined word or words to make the statement true.

6. Gamma rays, X-rays, ultraviolet radiation, visible light, infrared radiation, and radio waves make up the <u>Hertzsprung-Russell diagram</u>.
7. The sun is a <u>main-sequence</u> star.
8. Pulsars are a kind of <u>neutron star</u>.
9. More than half of all stars are <u>single</u> stars.
10. Acccording to the <u>big bang</u> theory, the universe has been growing for 10–15 billion years.

Checking Concepts

11. What types of radiation are included in the electromagnetic spectrum?
12. What kinds of information can astronomers obtain by studying the spectrum of a star?
13. Describe what will happen to the sun when it runs out of fuel.
14. Why can astronomers see the spiral arms of the Andromeda Galaxy more clearly than the spiral arms of the Milky Way Galaxy?
15. Describe the process by which the sun was formed.
16. **Writing to Learn** Imagine you have a spaceship that can travel much faster than the speed of light. Write a letter describing your three-part trip from Earth: to the nearest star other than the sun, to the center of our galaxy, and to the next nearest spiral galaxy.

Thinking Critically

17. **Relating Cause and Effect** Once every three days a small, bright star becomes much dimmer, only to return to its original brightness within six hours. Based on this information, what is causing the small star to become dimmer?
18. **Applying Concepts** Describe a real-world situation involving absolute and apparent magnitudes. (*Hint:* Think about riding in a car at night.)
19. **Comparing and Contrasting** Compare the life histories of a medium-mass star and a high-mass star. How are they similar? How are they different?
20. **Making Generalizations** What does knowing the rate at which the universe is expanding tell astronomers about the big bang?
21. **Applying Concepts** Is a light-year a unit of distance or a unit of time? Explain.

Applying Skills

Use the data about moving galaxies in the table below to answer Questions 22–24.

Cluster of Galaxies	Distance (millions of light-years)	Speed (kilometers per second)
Virgo	80	1,200
Ursa Major	980	15,000
Bootes	2,540	39,000
Hydra	3,980	61,000

22. **Graphing** Make a line graph showing how each cluster's distance from our galaxy is related to its speed. Put distance on the *x*-axis and speed on the *y*-axis.

23. **Interpreting Data** How are the distance and speed of a galaxy related?

24. **Drawing Conclusions** Does your graph indicate that the universe is expanding, contracting, or staying the same size? Explain.

Performance ▾ CHAPTER PROJECT 3 Assessment

Project Wrap Up Check the final draft of your story for correct spelling, grammar, punctuation, and usage. Make any necessary changes. Then decide how you will present your new constellation story. For example, you can make a poster showing the constellation, its star pattern, and your story. You can read your story aloud or perform it as a skit or play.

Reflect and Record This project has given you a chance to research information and then present it in writing. In your journal, write what you found easiest and hardest about researching and writing.

Test Preparation
Use these questions to prepare for standardized tests.

Study the diagram. Then answer Questions 25–29.

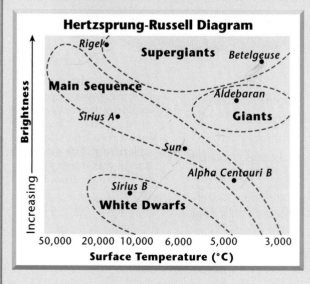

25. To which group do most stars belong?
    a. supergiants   **b.** giants
    c. main sequence   **d.** white dwarfs

26. Which star is hotter than the sun?
    a. Betelgeuse
    b. Aldebaran
    c. Alpha Centauri B
    d. Sirius B

27. Which star is most likely to be red?
    a. Rigel
    b. Sirius A
    c. Sirius B
    d. Betelgeuse

28. Compared to Rigel, Alpha Centauri B is
    a. cooler and brighter.
    b. cooler and dimmer.
    c. hotter and brighter.
    d. hotter and dimmer.

29. Which star has a greater absolute magnitude?
    a. Rigel
    b. Betelgeuse
    c. Sirius B
    d. Aldebaran

JOURNEY TO
MARS

The little six-wheeled rover inched down the steep ramp of the lander and onto the surface of Mars. Scientists on Earth held their breaths. Then, Sojourner hummed into action.

Sojourner became the star of the 1997 *Pathfinder* mission. Engineers at the Jet Propulsion Laboratory in Pasadena, California, guided the rover from remote controls on Earth. It rolled from rock to rock, collecting scientific data and checking the mineral content of each rock. Back on Earth, the *Pathfinder* team named the rocks after cartoon characters—Barnacle Bill, Scooby Doo, and Casper. They named a bear-shaped rock Yogi.

Pathfinder had landed in a region of Mars that no one had seen closely before. The lander took photographs of Martian landscapes, sunrises, and sunsets. Running on energy from solar panels, *Pathfinder's* instruments sent back huge amounts of information for scientists on Earth to analyze. This mission was just one of many that would study the Martian landscape.

Sojourner—about the size of a microwave oven—explores the rocky surface of Mars. Here it bumps into a rock that scientists called Yogi. The electronic image was transmitted by *Pathfinder* from Mars to Earth.

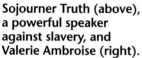

Sojourner Truth (above), a powerful speaker against slavery, and Valerie Ambroise (right).

Honor in a Name

Would you like to name a spacecraft? A 13-year-old student from Connecticut got that chance. Valerie Ambroise chose the name *Sojourner* for the small Pathfinder rover that explored the Martian surface in 1997. In a contest sponsored by NASA and The Planetary Society, Valerie wrote the winning essay for the best name. There were 3,500 student entries.

Valerie named *Sojourner* after Sojourner Truth, an African American reformer in the 1840s and 1850s. Here is Valerie Ambroise's essay.

The name of the Pathfinder should be Sojourner Truth. I chose Sojourner because she was a heroine to Blacks, slaves, and women. She acted on her strong feelings about life and the way it should be. Her greatest companions were God and her beliefs. Her greatest achievements included the book of her life written through her by a friend, meeting President Lincoln, meeting President Grant, her speeches and tours, her work at hospitals for soldiers during the Civil War, and her intellect (considering that she was illiterate). She went on many journeys and told many truths. She spoke with such eloquence that she moved people with simple words and understandings.

It's only logical that the Pathfinder be named Sojourner Truth, because she is on a journey to find truths about Mars. The Pathfinder should be able to have strong personalities in order to go under harsh conditions like that on Mars. Truth, while on tours, went under many harsh conditions. Even before, she went under harsh conditions as a slave.

Like Sojourner, the Pathfinder should be able to survive with what she already has. She should not need any extra equipment for surviving. The Pathfinder could use its feet like wheels, for transportation. Sojourner used her feet to travel a lot.

To research Mars, first, Sojourner would find out all she could about it. She always tried to understand further about what she was fighting for. When she got her information; she would use this information in Mars to study it more and add it to hers. She would act quickly to get what she wanted or what she felt was needed. Her talents in her work would be the same on Mars. She would use her eloquent voice and powerful actions.

You must admit, Sojourner and the Pathfinder are important.

Language Arts Activity

You have the chance to name the first research station on Mars, honoring an important person in scientific exploration or discovery. Research your hero or heroine. Then write a persuasive essay explaining why the research station should be named after him or her.

An artist imagines a scene in the future in which humans walk on the rocky plains of Mars.

Essentials for Survival

You step out of your spacecraft onto a dusty red landscape under a pinkish-red sky. Now you know why Mars is called the "red planet." Water vapor in the air forms thin clouds, even fog. Because the air is so thin, the sun glares down. It's windy, too. Thick clouds of reddish dust, rich in iron, blow around you.

Without a pressurized spacesuit, you would not survive in the thin Martian air. Unlike the thick layers of atmosphere around Earth, this atmosphere gives almost no protection against harmful ultraviolet radiation. You also must carry oxygen. Martian air is about 95 percent carbon dioxide, which humans can't breathe.

Your spacesuit must keep you warm. Even at the Martian equator, daytime temperatures are rarely above freezing. At night they plunge to about –100°C. Walk carefully, too, because Martian gravity is weak. You'll feel only 38 percent of your Earth weight!

This is a 360-degree image taken from *Pathfinder.* On the rugged Martian landscape, sand and dust storms have carved rocks into fantastic shapes. Deep canyons and huge volcanoes also shape the surface.

Science Activity

Plants grown in water   Plants grown in gravel

Plants — Wire mesh — Sand or gravel — Water — Plastic containers

Any human settlement on Mars would have to grow some of its own food. Experiment with a method called hydroponics—growing plants mainly in water, without soil. Set up two plant containers to grow tomatoes or peppers.

◆ Decide what variables to control.

◆ In one container, use just water and plant food, with a wire mesh support.

◆ In the other, add sand or gravel to root plants; add water and plant food.

◆ Record the rate of growth and strength of each plant over a two-to three-week period.

Which technique worked the best? How do you think hydroponics would work on Mars?

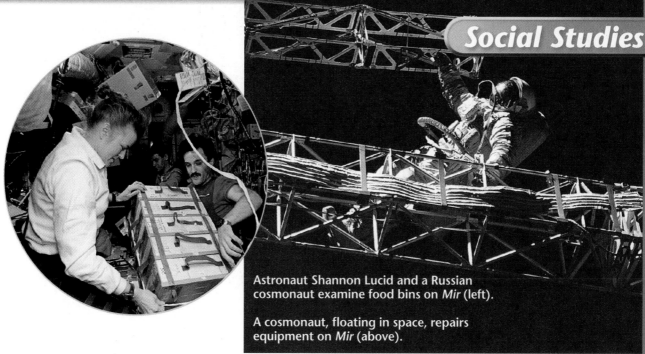

Astronaut Shannon Lucid and a Russian cosmonaut examine food bins on *Mir* (left).

A cosmonaut, floating in space, repairs equipment on *Mir* (above).

Partners in Space

Many engineers and scientists are confident that humans will travel to Mars sometime in the next 25 years. Meanwhile, people have gotten a preview of a space voyage from astronauts and cosmonauts traveling on space shuttles, on *Mir*, Russia's former space station, and on the new International Space Station.

For years, the United States and the Soviet Union competed in a race to send missions into space. Beginning in 1997, Russia and the United States cooperated on *Mir*. Americans worked with cosmonauts to solve problems, make repairs, take spacewalks, and run the ship's computers. More recently, scientists from 16 countries have cooperated to construct and operate the International Space Station, which is being built in orbit.

What's it like for crew members from different backgrounds to live and work together in a cramped spacecraft? Besides having cultural and language differences, Russian and American crews have different training and different equipment. Even spacesuits are not the same.

Because *Mir* was an old station, space crews gained experience dealing with emergencies. On a long flight, such as one to Mars, those skills would be essential.

All this experience on *Mir* and the International Space Station should prove invaluable for a future expedition to Mars.

Social Studies Activity

The first trips to Mars will probably take at least 6 to 8 months. Think about the difficulties you would have spending 7 months in a spacecraft about the size of a school bus. Set up rules and guidelines for your voyage. Plan for five astronauts from two different countries. Consider these issues:

◆ who will make decisions and give orders
◆ how you will communicate
◆ how you'll adjust for different living habits and backgrounds
◆ how you'll avoid getting bored
◆ how you'll resolve conflicts among crew members or with mission-control scientists on Earth.

Sols of Mars

Mars is the planet most like Earth. But its smaller size, greater distance from the sun, and different orbit cause some immense differences. A Martian day, called a sol, is only about 40 minutes longer than an Earth day. The Martian year, however, is much longer—669 sols.

Mars, like Earth, tilts on its axis, so it has seasons. Each Martian season lasts longer than an Earth season because the Martian year is longer. The shape of Mars's orbit makes the seasons unequal in length (see table below).

The climate in the southern hemisphere is more extreme than in the northern hemisphere. Winters in the south are longer and colder, while summers are shorter and warmer. Winter in the south, for instance, lasts 177 sols. In the northern hemisphere, winter lasts only 156 sols.

Seasonal changes affect Mars's north and south poles, which are covered with polar ice caps made of water and carbon dioxide. During winter in the southern hemisphere, the polar cap covers almost half the hemisphere. Here the ice cap is mainly frozen carbon dioxide—like dry ice. In spring, the ice cap partially melts, releasing carbon dioxide into the air. In a similar way, when spring comes in the northern hemisphere, the north polar cap melts. But in the north, the frozen core is made mainly of water ice.

An ice cap covers the northern polar region of Mars.

Northern Hemisphere of Mars

23%

27%

Winter   Summer

?   ?

Martian Seasons in Sols (Martian Days)		
	Northern Hemisphere	Southern Hemisphere
Winter	156	177
Spring	194	142
Summer	177	156
Fall	142	194

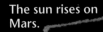

The sun rises on Mars.

Southern Hemisphere of Mars

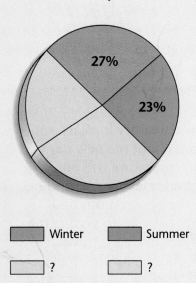

27%

23%

Winter   Summer

?   ?

Math Activity

People working on Mars would probably go by Martian time. You know that there are 669 sols (Martian days) in a Martian year. Knowing the number of sols in a season, you can figure the percent of the year that's winter. For example, winter in the northern hemisphere is 156 sols ÷ 669 sols ≈ 0.233 ≈ 23%.

◆ Use the table on page 132 to figure out what percent of the Martian year in each hemisphere is winter, spring, summer, and fall. Round to the nearest hundredth.

◆ Make two circle graphs like those on pages 132 and 133. Label, color, and write the percent for each season in the northern and southern hemispheres.

◆ Choose a different color for each.

If you had a choice, which hemisphere would you choose to live in?

Tie It Together

Plan a Martian Station

At last, you will be going to Mars to set up the first human research station. For an expedition this long, good planning is essential. Review the major problems that Mars presents to humans, such as thin atmosphere, no oxygen, extreme temperatures, and so on. Remember that it's too expensive to send most supplies to Mars. Work in groups to make a plan for setting up Earth's research station. Include maps and drawings. As you make your plan, consider questions such as these:

◆ How will you supply oxygen? Water? Fuel?

◆ What site will you choose for your settlement? Consider the landscape and climate on Mars.

◆ What supplies will you bring with you?

◆ What will you use for building materials?

◆ What kinds of food will you get? How will you get food?

This painting shows how one artist imagined a human home on another planet.

Think Like a Scientist

*A*lthough you may not know it, you think like a scientist every day. Whenever you ask a question and explore possible answers, you use many of the same skills that scientists do. Some of these skills are described on this page.

Observing

When you use one or more of your five senses to gather information about the world, you are **observing.** Hearing a dog bark, counting twelve green seeds, and smelling smoke are all observations. To increase the power of their senses, scientists sometimes use microscopes, telescopes, or other instruments that help them make more detailed observations.

An observation must be an accurate report of what your senses detect. It is important to keep careful records of your observations in science class by writing or drawing in a notebook. The information collected through observations is called evidence, or data.

Inferring

When you interpret an observation, you are **inferring,** or making an inference. For example, if you hear your dog barking, you may infer that someone is at your front door. To make this inference, you combine the evidence—the barking dog—and your experience or knowledge—you know that your dog barks when strangers approach—to reach a logical conclusion.

Notice that an inference is not a fact; it is only one of many possible interpretations for an observation. For example, your dog may be barking because it wants to go for a walk. An inference may turn out to be incorrect even if it is based on accurate observations and logical reasoning. The only way to find out if an inference is correct is to investigate further.

Predicting

When you listen to the weather forecast, you hear many predictions about the next day's weather—what the temperature will be, whether it will rain, and how windy it will be. Weather forecasters use observations and knowledge of weather patterns to predict the weather. The skill of **predicting** involves making an inference about a future event based on current evidence or past experience.

Because a prediction is an inference, it may prove to be false. In science class, you can test some of your predictions by doing experiments. For example, suppose you predict that larger paper airplanes can fly farther than smaller airplanes. How could you test your prediction?

ACTIVITY Use the photograph to answer the questions below.

Observing Look closely at the photograph. List at least three observations.

Inferring Use your observations to make an inference about what has happened. What experience or knowledge did you use to make the inference?

Predicting Predict what will happen next. On what evidence or experience do you base your prediction?

Classifying

Could you imagine searching for a book in the library if the books were shelved in no particular order? Your trip to the library would be an all-day event! Luckily, librarians group together books on similar topics or by the same author. Grouping together items that are alike in some way is called **classifying.** You can classify items in many ways: by size, by shape, by use, and by other important characteristics.

Like librarians, scientists use the skill of classifying to organize information and objects. When things are sorted into groups, the relationships among them become easier to understand.

ACTIVITY

Classify the objects in the photograph into two groups based on any characteristic you choose. Then use another characteristic to classify the objects into three groups.

Making Models

Have you ever drawn a picture to help someone understand what you were saying? Such a drawing is one type of model. A model is a picture, diagram, computer image, or other representation of a complex object or process. **Making models** helps people understand things that they cannot observe directly.

Scientists often use models to represent things that are either very large or very small, such as the planets in the solar system, or the parts of a cell. Such models are physical models—drawings or three-dimensional structures that look like the real thing. Other models are mental models—mathematical equations or words that describe how something works.

ACTIVITY

This student is using a model to demonstrate what causes day and night on Earth. What do the flashlight and the tennis ball in the model represent?

Communicating

Whenever you talk on the phone, write a letter, or listen to your teacher at school, you are communicating. **Communicating** is the process of sharing ideas and information with other people. Communicating effectively requires many skills, including writing, reading, speaking, listening, and making models.

Scientists communicate to share results, information, and opinions. Scientists often communicate about their work in journals, over the telephone, in letters, and on the Internet. They also attend scientific meetings where they share their ideas with one another in person.

ACTIVITY

On a sheet of paper, write out clear, detailed directions for tying your shoe. Then exchange directions with a partner. Follow your partner's directions exactly. How successful were you at tying your shoe? How could your partner have communicated more clearly?

Making Measurements

When scientists make observations, it is not sufficient to say that something is "big" or "heavy." Instead, scientists use instruments to measure just how big or heavy an object is. By measuring, scientists can express their observations more precisely and communicate more information about what they observe.

Measuring in SI

The standard system of measurement used by scientists around the world is known as the International System of Units, which is abbreviated as SI (in French, *Système International d'Unités*). SI units are easy to use because they are based on multiples of 10. Each unit is ten times larger than the next smallest unit and one tenth the size of the next largest unit. The table lists the prefixes used to name the most common SI units.

Common SI Prefixes

Prefix	Symbol	Meaning
kilo-	k	1,000
hecto-	h	100
deka-	da	10
deci-	d	0.1 (one tenth)
centi-	c	0.01 (one hundredth)
milli-	m	0.001 (one thousandth)

Length To measure length, or the distance between two points, the unit of measure is the **meter (m).** The distance from the floor to a doorknob is approximately one meter. Long distances, such as the distance between two cities, are measured in kilometers (km). Small lengths are measured in centimeters (cm) or millimeters (mm). Scientists use metric rulers and meter sticks to measure length.

Common Conversions

1 km = 1,000 m
1 m = 100 cm
1 m = 1,000 mm
1 cm = 10 mm

The larger lines on the metric ruler in the picture show centimeter divisions, while the smaller, unnumbered lines show millimeter divisions. How many centimeters long is the shell? How many millimeters long is it?

ACTIVITY

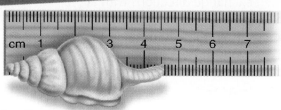

Liquid Volume To measure the volume of a liquid, or the amount of space it takes up, you will use a unit of measure known as the **liter (L).** One liter is the approximate volume of a medium-size carton of milk. Smaller volumes are measured in milliliters (mL). Scientists use graduated cylinders to measure liquid volume.

Common Conversion

1 L = 1,000 mL

The graduated cylinder in the picture is marked in milliliter divisions. Notice that the water in the cylinder has a curved surface. This curved surface is called the *meniscus.* To measure the volume, you must read the level at the lowest point of the meniscus. What is the volume of water in this graduated cylinder?

ACTIVITY

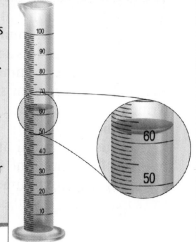

Mass To measure mass, or the amount of matter in an object, you will use a unit of measure known as the **gram (g)**. One gram is approximately the mass of a paper clip. Larger masses are measured in kilograms (kg). Scientists use a balance to find the mass of an object.

Common Conversion

1 kg = 1,000 g

The mass of the apple in the picture is measured in kilograms. What is the mass of the apple? Suppose a recipe for applesauce called for one kilogram of apples. About how many apples would you need?

Temperature
To measure the temperature of a substance, you will use the **Celsius scale**. Temperature is measured in degrees Celsius (°C) using a Celsius thermometer. Water freezes at 0°C and boils at 100°C.

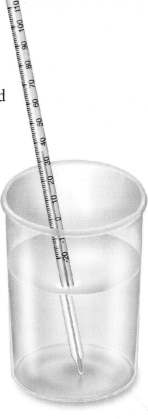

ACTIVITY
What is the temperature of the liquid in degrees Celsius?

Converting SI Units

To use the SI system, you must know how to convert between units. Converting from one unit to another involves the skill of **calculating**, or using mathematical operations. Converting between SI units is similar to converting between dollars and dimes because both systems are based on multiples of ten.

Suppose you want to convert a length of 80 centimeters to meters. Follow these steps to convert between units.

1. Begin by writing down the measurement you want to convert—in this example, 80 centimeters.
2. Write a conversion factor that represents the relationship between the two units you are converting. In this example, the relationship is *1 meter = 100 centimeters*. Write this conversion factor as a fraction, making sure to place the units you are converting from (centimeters, in this example) in the denominator.

3. Multiply the measurement you want to convert by the fraction. When you do this, the units in the first measurement will cancel out with the units in the denominator. Your answer will be in the units you are converting to (meters, in this example).

Example

80 centimeters = ___?___ meters

$$80 \text{ centimeters} \times \frac{1 \text{ meter}}{100 \text{ centimeters}} = \frac{80 \text{ meters}}{100}$$

$$= 0.8 \text{ meters}$$

Convert between the following units.
1. 600 millimeters = _?_ meters
2. 0.35 liters = _?_ milliliters
3. 1,050 grams = _?_ kilograms

Conducting a Scientific Investigation

In some ways, scientists are like detectives, piecing together clues to learn about a process or event. One way that scientists gather clues is by carrying out experiments. An experiment tests an idea in a careful, orderly manner. Although experiments do not all follow the same steps in the same order, many follow a pattern similar to the one described here.

Posing Questions

Experiments begin by asking a scientific question. A scientific question is one that can be answered by gathering evidence. For example, the question "Which freezes faster—fresh water or salt water?" is a scientific question because you can carry out an investigation and gather information to answer the question.

Developing a Hypothesis

The next step is to form a hypothesis. A **hypothesis** is a possible explanation for a set of observations or answer to a scientific question. In science, a hypothesis must be something that can be tested. A hypothesis can be worded as an *If…then…* statement. For example, a hypothesis might be *"If I add salt to fresh water, then the water will take longer to freeze."* A hypothesis worded this way serves as a rough outline of the experiment you should perform.

Designing an Experiment

Next you need to plan a way to test your hypothesis. Your plan should be written out as a step-by-step procedure and should describe the observations or measurements you will make.

Two important steps involved in designing an experiment are controlling variables and forming operational definitions.

Controlling Variables In a well-designed experiment, you need to keep all variables the same except for one. A **variable** is any factor that can change in an experiment. The factor that you change is called the **manipulated variable.** In this experiment, the manipulated variable is the amount of salt added to the water. Other factors, such as the amount of water or the starting temperature, are kept constant.

The factor that changes as a result of the manipulated variable is called the responding variable. The **responding variable** is what you measure or observe to obtain your results. In this experiment, the responding variable is how long the water takes to freeze.

An experiment in which all factors except one are kept constant is a **controlled experiment.** Most controlled experiments include a test called the control. In this experiment, Container 3 is the control. Because no salt is added to Container 3, you can compare the results from the other containers to it. Any difference in results must be due to the addition of salt alone.

Forming Operational Definitions Another important aspect of a well-designed experiment is having clear operational definitions. An **operational definition** is a statement that describes how a particular variable is to be measured or how a term is to be defined. For example, in this experiment, how will you determine if the water has frozen? You might decide to insert a stick in each container at the start of the experiment. Your operational definition of "frozen" would be the time at which the stick can no longer move.

EXPERIMENTAL PROCEDURE

1. Fill 3 containers with 300 milliliters of cold tap water.

2. Add 10 grams of salt to Container 1; stir. Add 20 grams of salt to Container 2; stir. Add no salt to Container 3.

3. Place the 3 containers in a freezer.

4. Check the containers every 15 minutes. Record your observations.

Interpreting Data

The observations and measurements you make in an experiment are called data. At the end of an experiment, you need to analyze the data to look for any patterns or trends. Patterns often become clear if you organize your data in a data table or graph. Then think through what the data reveal. Do they support your hypothesis? Do they point out a flaw in your experiment? Do you need to collect more data?

Drawing Conclusions

A conclusion is a statement that sums up what you have learned from an experiment. When you draw a conclusion, you need to decide whether the data you collected support your hypothesis or not. You may need to repeat an experiment several times before you can draw any conclusions from it. Conclusions often lead you to pose new questions and plan new experiments to answer them.

Is a ball's bounce affected by the height from which it is dropped? Using the steps just described, plan a controlled experiment to investigate this problem. **ACTIVITY**

Thinking Critically

Has a friend ever asked for your advice about a problem? If so, you may have helped your friend think through the problem in a logical way. Without knowing it, you used critical-thinking skills to help your friend. Critical thinking involves the use of reasoning and logic to solve problems or make decisions. Some critical-thinking skills are described below.

Comparing and Contrasting

When you examine two objects for similarities and differences, you are using the skill of **comparing and contrasting.** Comparing involves identifying similarities, or common characteristics. Contrasting involves identifying differences. Analyzing objects in this way can help you discover details that you might otherwise overlook.

ACTIVITY
Compare and contrast the two animals in the photo. First list all the similarities that you see. Then list all the differences.

Applying Concepts

When you use your knowledge about one situation to make sense of a similar situation, you are using the skill of **applying concepts.** Being able to transfer your knowledge from one situation to another shows that you truly understand a concept. You may use this skill in answering test questions that present different problems from the ones you've reviewed in class.

ACTIVITY
You have just learned that water takes longer to freeze when other substances are mixed into it. Use this knowledge to explain why people need a substance called antifreeze in their car's radiator in the winter.

Interpreting Illustrations

Diagrams, photographs, and maps are included in textbooks to help clarify what you read. These illustrations show processes, places, and ideas in a visual manner. The skill called **interpreting illustrations** can help you learn from these visual elements. To understand an illustration, take the time to study the illustration along with all the written information that accompanies it. Captions identify the key concepts shown in the illustration. Labels point out the important parts of a diagram or map, while keys identify the symbols used in a map.

Bristles

Upper blood vessel

Reproductive organs

Arches

Brain

Mouth

Digestive tract

Lower blood vessel

Nerve cord

Waste-removal organs

Intestine

▲ **Internal anatomy of an earthworm**

ACTIVITY
Study the diagram above. Then write a short paragraph explaining what you have learned.

Relating Cause and Effect

If one event causes another event to occur, the two events are said to have a cause-and-effect relationship. When you determine that such a relationship exists between two events, you use a skill called **relating cause and effect.** For example, if you notice an itchy, red bump on your skin, you might infer that a mosquito bit you. The mosquito bite is the cause, and the bump is the effect.

It is important to note that two events do not necessarily have a cause-and-effect relationship just because they occur together. Scientists carry out experiments or use past experience to determine whether a cause-and-effect relationship exists.

ACTIVITY

You are on a camping trip and your flashlight has stopped working. List some possible causes for the flashlight malfunction. How could you determine which cause-and-effect relationship has left you in the dark?

Making Generalizations

When you draw a conclusion about an entire group based on information about only some of the group's members, you are using a skill called **making generalizations.** For a generalization to be valid, the sample you choose must be large enough and representative of the entire group. You might, for example, put this skill to work at a farm stand if you see a sign that says, "Sample some grapes before you buy." If you sample a few sweet grapes, you may conclude that all the grapes are sweet—and purchase a large bunch.

ACTIVITY

A team of scientists needs to determine whether the water in a large reservoir is safe to drink. How could they use the skill of making generalizations to help them? What should they do?

Making Judgments

When you evaluate something to decide whether it is good or bad, or right or wrong, you are using a skill called **making judgments.** For example, you make judgments when you decide to eat healthful foods or to pick up litter in a park. Before you make a judgment, you need to think through the pros and cons of a situation, and identify the values or standards that you hold.

ACTIVITY

Should children and teens be required to wear helmets when bicycling? Explain why you feel the way you do.

Problem Solving

When you use critical-thinking skills to resolve an issue or decide on a course of action, you are using a skill called **problem solving.** Some problems, such as how to convert a fraction into a decimal, are straightforward. Other problems, such as figuring out why your computer has stopped working, are complex. Some complex problems can be solved using the trial and error method—try out one solution first, and if that doesn't work, try another. Other useful problem-solving strategies include making models and brainstorming possible solutions with a partner.

Organizing Information

As you read this textbook, how can you make sense of all the information it contains? Some useful tools to help you organize information are shown on this page. These tools are called *graphic organizers* because they give you a visual picture of a topic, showing at a glance how key concepts are related.

Concept Maps

Concept maps are useful tools for organizing information on broad topics. A concept map begins with a general concept and shows how it can be broken down into more specific concepts. In that way, relationships between concepts become easier to understand.

A concept map is constructed by placing concept words (usually nouns) in ovals and connecting them with linking words. Often, the most general concept word is placed at the top, and the words become more specific as you move downward. Often the linking words, which are written on a line extending between two ovals, describe the relationship between the two concepts they connect. If you follow any string of concepts and linking words down the map, it should read like a sentence.

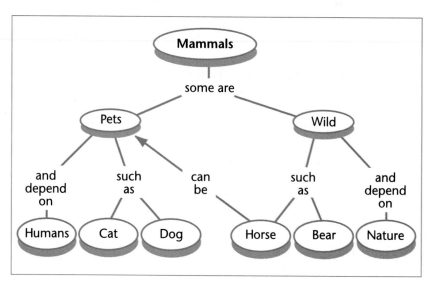

Some concept maps include linking words that connect a concept on one branch of the map to a concept on another branch. These linking words, called cross-linkages, show more complex interrelationships among concepts.

Compare/Contrast Tables

Compare/contrast tables are useful tools for sorting out the similarities and differences between two or more items. A table provides an organized framework in which to compare items based on specific characteristics that you identify.

To create a compare/contrast table, list the items to be compared across the top of a table. Then list the characteristics that will form the basis of your comparison in the left-hand

Characteristic	Baseball	Basketball
Number of Players	9	5
Playing Field	Baseball diamond	Basketball court
Equipment	Bat, baseball, mitts	Basket, basketball

column. Complete the table by filling in information about each characteristic, first for one item and then for the other.

Venn Diagrams

Another way to show similarities and differences between items is with a Venn diagram. A Venn diagram consists of two or more circles that partially overlap. Each circle represents a particular concept or idea. Common characteristics, or similarities, are written within the area of overlap between the two circles. Unique characteristics, or differences, are written in the parts of the circles outside the area of overlap.

To create a Venn diagram, draw two overlapping circles. Label the circles with the names of the items being compared. Write the

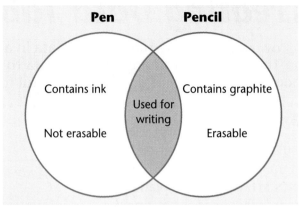

unique characteristics in each circle outside the area of overlap. Then write the shared characteristics within the area of overlap.

Flowcharts

A flowchart can help you understand the order in which certain events have occurred or should occur. Flowcharts are useful for outlining the stages in a process or the steps in a procedure.

To make a flowchart, write a brief description of each event in a box. Place the first event at the top of the page, followed by the second event, the third event, and so on. Then draw an arrow to connect each event to the one that occurs next.

Preparing Pasta

Boil water

↓

Cook pasta

↓

Drain water

↓

Add sauce

Cycle Diagrams

A cycle diagram can be used to show a sequence of events that is continuous, or cyclical. A continuous sequence does not have an end because, when the final event is over, the first event begins again. Like a flowchart, a cycle diagram can help you understand the order of events.

To create a cycle diagram, write a brief description of each event in a box. Place one event at the top of the page in the center. Then, moving in a clockwise direction around an imaginary circle, write each event in its proper sequence. Draw arrows that connect each event to the one that occurs next, forming a continuous circle.

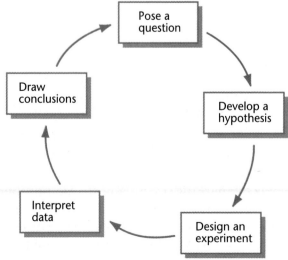

Steps in a Science Experiment

Creating Data Tables and Graphs

How can you make sense of the data in a science experiment? The first step is to organize the data to help you understand them. Data tables and graphs are helpful tools for organizing data.

Data Tables

You have gathered your materials and set up your experiment. But before you start, you need to plan a way to record what happens during the experiment. By creating a data table, you can record your observations and measurements in an orderly way.

Suppose, for example, that a scientist conducted an experiment to find out how many Calories people of different body masses burn while doing various activities. The data table shows the results.

Notice in this data table that the manipulated variable (body mass) is the heading of one column. The responding

CALORIES BURNED IN 30 MINUTES OF ACTIVITY			
Body Mass	Experiment 1 Bicycling	Experiment 2 Playing Basketball	Experiment 3 Watching Television
30 kg	60 Calories	120 Calories	21 Calories
40 kg	77 Calories	164 Calories	27 Calories
50 kg	95 Calories	206 Calories	33 Calories
60 kg	114 Calories	248 Calories	38 Calories

variable (for Experiment 1, the number of Calories burned while bicycling) is the heading of the next column. Additional columns were added for related experiments.

Bar Graphs

To compare how many Calories a person burns doing various activities, you could create a bar graph. A bar graph is used to display data in a number of separate, or distinct, categories. In this example, bicycling, playing basketball, and watching television are three separate categories.

To create a bar graph, follow these steps.

1. On graph paper, draw a horizontal, or *x*-, axis and a vertical, or *y*-, axis.
2. Write the names of the categories to be graphed along the horizontal axis. Include an overall label for the axis as well.
3. Label the vertical axis with the name of the responding variable. Include units of measurement. Then create a scale along the axis by marking off equally spaced numbers that cover the range of the data collected.
4. For each category, draw a solid bar using the scale on the vertical axis to determine the

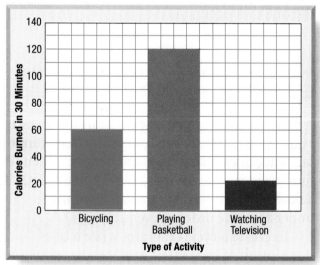

Calories Burned by a 30-kilogram Person in Various Activities

appropriate height. For example, for bicycling, draw the bar as high as the 60 mark on the vertical axis. Make all the bars the same width and leave equal spaces between them.
5. Add a title that describes the graph.

Line Graphs

To see whether a relationship exists between body mass and the number of Calories burned while bicycling, you could create a line graph. A line graph is used to display data that show how one variable (the responding variable) changes in response to another variable (the manipulated variable). You can use a line graph when your manipulated variable is *continuous*, that is, when there are other points between the ones that you tested. In this example, body mass is a continuous variable because there are other body masses between 30 and 40 kilograms (for example, 31 kilograms). Time is another example of a continuous variable.

Line graphs are powerful tools because they allow you to estimate values for conditions that you did not test in the experiment. For example, you can use the line graph to estimate that a 35-kilogram person would burn 68 Calories while bicycling.

To create a line graph, follow these steps.

1. On graph paper, draw a horizontal, or *x*-, axis and a vertical, or *y*-, axis.
2. Label the horizontal axis with the name of the manipulated variable. Label the vertical axis with the name of the responding variable. Include units of measurement.
3. Create a scale on each axis by marking off equally spaced numbers that cover the range of the data collected.
4. Plot a point on the graph for each piece of data. In the line graph above, the dotted lines show how to plot the first data point (30 kilograms and 60 Calories). Draw an imaginary vertical line extending up from the horizontal axis at the 30-kilogram mark. Then draw an imaginary horizontal line extending across from the vertical axis at the 60-Calorie mark. Plot the point where the two lines intersect.

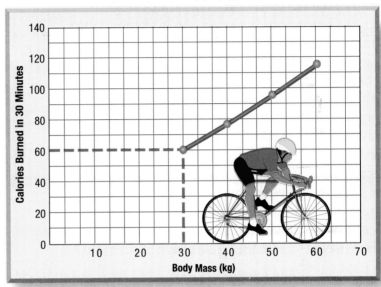

Effect of Body Mass on Calories Burned While Bicycling

5. Connect the plotted points with a solid line. (In some cases, it may be more appropriate to draw a line that shows the general trend of the plotted points. In those cases, some of the points may fall above or below the line. Also, not all graphs are linear. It may be more appropriate to draw a curve to connect the points.)
6. Add a title that identifies the variables or relationship in the graph.

Create line graphs to display the data from Experiment 2 and Experiment 3 in the data table. **ACTIVITY**

You read in the newspaper that a total of 4 centimeters of rain fell in your area in June, 2.5 centimeters fell in July, and 1.5 centimeters fell in August. What type of graph would you use to display these data? Use graph paper to create the graph. **ACTIVITY**

Circle Graphs

Like bar graphs, circle graphs can be used to display data in a number of separate categories. Unlike bar graphs, however, circle graphs can only be used when you have data for *all* the categories that make up a given topic. A circle graph is sometimes called a pie chart because it resembles a pie cut into slices. The pie represents the entire topic, while the slices represent the individual categories. The size of a slice indicates what percentage of the whole a particular category makes up.

The data table below shows the results of a survey in which 24 teenagers were asked to identify their favorite sport. The data were then used to create the circle graph at the right.

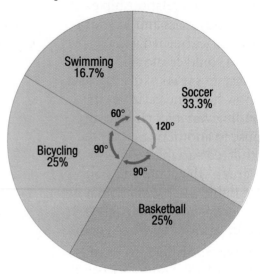

Sports That Teens Prefer

FAVORITE SPORTS

Sport	Number of Students
Soccer	8
Basketball	6
Bicycling	6
Swimming	4

To create a circle graph, follow these steps.

1. Use a compass to draw a circle. Mark the center of the circle with a point. Then draw a line from the center point to the top of the circle.
2. Determine the size of each "slice" by setting up a proportion where x equals the number of degrees in a slice. (NOTE: A circle contains 360 degrees.) For example, to find the number of degrees in the "soccer" slice, set up the following proportion:

$$\frac{\text{students who prefer soccer}}{\text{total number of students}} = \frac{x}{\text{total number of degrees in a circle}}$$

$$\frac{8}{24} = \frac{x}{360}$$

Cross-multiply and solve for x.

$$24x = 8 \times 360$$
$$x = 120$$

The "soccer" slice should contain 120 degrees.

3. Use a protractor to measure the angle of the first slice, using the line you drew to the top of the circle as the 0° line. Draw a line from the center of the circle to the edge for the angle you measured.
4. Continue around the circle by measuring the size of each slice with the protractor. Start measuring from the edge of the previous slice so the wedges do not overlap. When you are done, the entire circle should be filled in.
5. Determine the percentage of the whole circle that each slice represents. To do this, divide the number of degrees in a slice by the total number of degrees in a circle (360), and multiply by 100%. For the "soccer" slice, you can find the percentage as follows:

$$\frac{120}{360} \times 100\% = 33.3\%$$

6. Use a different color to shade in each slice. Label each slice with the name of the category and with the percentage of the whole it represents.
7. Add a title to the circle graph.

ACTIVITY

In a class of 28 students, 12 students take the bus to school, 10 students walk, and 6 students ride their bicycles. Create a circle graph to display these data.

Laboratory Safety

Safety Symbols

These symbols alert you to possible dangers in the laboratory and remind you to work carefully.

Safety Goggles Always wear safety goggles to protect your eyes in any activity involving chemicals, flames or heating, or the possibility of broken glassware.

Lab Apron Wear a laboratory apron to protect your skin and clothing from damage.

Breakage You are working with materials that may be breakable, such as glass containers, glass tubing, thermometers, or funnels. Handle breakable materials with care. Do not touch broken glassware.

Heat-resistant Gloves Use an oven mitt or other hand protection when handling hot materials. Hot plates, hot glassware, or hot water can cause burns. Do not touch hot objects with your bare hands.

Heating Use a clamp or tongs to pick up hot glassware. Do not touch hot objects with your bare hands.

Sharp Object Pointed-tip scissors, scalpels, knives, needles, pins, or tacks are sharp. They can cut or puncture your skin. Always direct a sharp edge or point away from yourself and others. Use sharp instruments only as instructed.

Electric Shock Avoid the possibility of electric shock. Never use electrical equipment around water, or when the equipment is wet or your hands are wet. Be sure cords are untangled and cannot trip anyone. Disconnect the equipment when it is not in use.

Corrosive Chemical You are working with an acid or another corrosive chemical. Avoid getting it on your skin or clothing, or in your eyes. Do not inhale the vapors. Wash your hands when you are finished with the activity.

Poison Do not let any poisonous chemical come in contact with your skin, and do not inhale its vapors. Wash your hands when you are finished with the activity.

Physical Safety When an experiment involves physical activity, take precautions to avoid injuring yourself or others. Follow instructions from your teacher. Alert your teacher if there is any reason you should not participate in the activity.

Animal Safety Treat live animals with care to avoid harming the animals or yourself. Working with animal parts or preserved animals also may require caution. Wash your hands when you are finished with the activity.

Plant Safety Handle plants in the laboratory or during field work only as directed by your teacher. If you are allergic to certain plants, tell your teacher before doing an activity in which those plants are used. Avoid touching harmful plants such as poison ivy, poison oak, or poison sumac, or plants with thorns. Wash your hands when you are finished with the activity.

Flames You may be working with flames from a lab burner, candle, or matches. Tie back loose hair and clothing. Follow instructions from your teacher about lighting and extinguishing flames.

No Flames Flammable materials may be present. Make sure there are no flames, sparks, or other exposed heat sources present.

Fumes When poisonous or unpleasant vapors may be involved, work in a ventilated area. Avoid inhaling vapors directly. Only test an odor when directed to do so by your teacher, and use a wafting motion to direct the vapor toward your nose.

Disposal Chemicals and other laboratory materials used in the activity must be disposed of safely. Follow the instructions from your teacher.

Hand Washing Wash your hands thoroughly when finished with the activity. Use antibacterial soap and warm water. Lather both sides of your hands and between your fingers. Rinse well.

General Safety Awareness You may see this symbol when none of the symbols described earlier appears. In this case, follow the specific instructions provided. You may also see this symbol when you are asked to develop your own procedure in a lab. Have your teacher approve your plan before you go further.

Science Safety Rules

To prepare yourself to work safely in the laboratory, read over the following safety rules. Then read them a second time. Make sure you understand and follow each rule. Ask your teacher to explain any rules you do not understand.

Dress Code

1. To protect yourself from injuring your eyes, wear safety goggles whenever you work with chemicals, burners, glassware, or any substance that might get into your eyes. If you wear contact lenses, notify your teacher.
2. Wear a lab apron or coat whenever you work with corrosive chemicals or substances that can stain.
3. Tie back long hair to keep it away from any chemicals, flames, or equipment.
4. Remove or tie back any article of clothing or jewelry that can hang down and touch chemicals, flames, or equipment. Roll up or secure long sleeves.
5. Never wear open shoes or sandals.

General Precautions

6. Read all directions for an experiment several times before beginning the activity. Carefully follow all written and oral instructions. If you are in doubt about any part of the experiment, ask your teacher for assistance.
7. Never perform activities that are not assigned or authorized by your teacher. Obtain permission before "experimenting" on your own. Never handle any equipment unless you have specific permission.
8. Never perform lab activities without direct supervision.
9. Never eat or drink in the laboratory.
10. Keep work areas clean and tidy at all times. Bring only notebooks and lab manuals or written lab procedures to the work area. All other items, such as purses and backpacks, should be left in a designated area.
11. Do not engage in horseplay.

First Aid

12. Always report all accidents or injuries to your teacher, no matter how minor. Notify your teacher immediately about any fires.
13. Learn what to do in case of specific accidents, such as getting acid in your eyes or on your skin. (Rinse acids from your body with lots of water.)
14. Be aware of the location of the first-aid kit, but do not use it unless instructed by your teacher. In case of injury, your teacher should administer first aid. Your teacher may also send you to the school nurse or call a physician.
15. Know the location of emergency equipment, such as the fire extinguisher and fire blanket, and know how to use it.
16. Know the location of the nearest telephone and whom to contact in an emergency.

Heating and Fire Safety

17. Never use a heat source, such as a candle, burner, or hot plate, without wearing safety goggles.
18. Never heat anything unless instructed to do so. A chemical that is harmless when cool may be dangerous when heated.
19. Keep all combustible materials away from flames. Never use a flame or spark near a combustible chemical.
20. Never reach across a flame.
21. Before using a laboratory burner, make sure you know proper procedures for lighting and adjusting the burner, as demonstrated by your teacher. Do not touch the burner. It may be hot. And never leave a lighted burner unattended!
22. Chemicals can splash or boil out of a heated test tube. When heating a substance in a test tube, make sure that the mouth of the tube is not pointed at you or anyone else.
23. Never heat a liquid in a closed container. The expanding gases produced may blow the container apart.
24. Before picking up a container that has been heated, hold the back of your hand near it. If you can feel heat on the back of your hand, the container is too hot to handle. Use an oven mitt to pick up a container that has been heated.

Using Chemicals Safely

25. Never mix chemicals "for the fun of it." You might produce a dangerous, possibly explosive substance.

26. Never put your face near the mouth of a container that holds chemicals. Many chemicals are poisonous. Never touch, taste, or smell a chemical unless you are instructed by your teacher to do so.

27. Use only those chemicals needed in the activity. Read and double-check labels on supply bottles before removing any chemicals. Take only as much as you need. Keep all containers closed when chemicals are not being used.

28. Dispose of all chemicals as instructed by your teacher. To avoid contamination, never return chemicals to their original containers. Never simply pour chemicals or other substances into the sink or trash containers.

29. Be extra careful when working with acids or bases. Pour all chemicals over the sink or a container, not over your work surface.

30. If you are instructed to test for odors, use a wafting motion to direct the odors to your nose. Do not inhale the fumes directly from the container.

31. When mixing an acid and water, always pour the water into the container first and then add the acid to the water. Never pour water into an acid.

32. Take extreme care not to spill any material in the laboratory. Wash chemical spills and splashes immediately with plenty of water. Immediately begin rinsing with water any acids that get on your skin or clothing, and notify your teacher of any acid spill at the same time.

Using Glassware Safely

33. Never force glass tubing or thermometers into a rubber stopper or rubber tubing. Have your teacher insert the glass tubing or thermometer if required for an activity.

34. If you are using a laboratory burner, use a wire screen to protect glassware from any flame. Never heat glassware that is not thoroughly dry on the outside.

35. Keep in mind that hot glassware looks cool. Never pick up glassware without first checking to see if it is hot. Use an oven mitt. See rule 24.

36. Never use broken or chipped glassware. If glassware breaks, notify your teacher and dispose of the glassware in the proper broken-glassware container. Never handle broken glass with your bare hands.

37. Never eat or drink from lab glassware.

38. Thoroughly clean glassware before putting it away.

Using Sharp Instruments

39. Handle scalpels or other sharp instruments with extreme care. Never cut material toward you; cut away from you.

40. Immediately notify your teacher if you cut your skin when working in the laboratory.

Animal and Plant Safety

41. Never perform experiments that cause pain, discomfort, or harm to animals. This rule applies at home as well as in the classroom.

42. Animals should be handled only if absolutely necessary. Your teacher will instruct you as to how to handle each animal species brought into the classroom.

43. If you know that you are allergic to certain plants, molds, or animals, tell your teacher before doing an activity in which these are used.

44. During field work, protect your skin by wearing long pants, long sleeves, socks, and closed shoes. Know how to recognize the poisonous plants and fungi in your area, as well as plants with thorns, and avoid contact with them. Never eat any part of a plant or fungus.

45. Wash your hands thoroughly after handling animals or a cage containing animals. Wash your hands when you are finished with any activity involving animal parts, plants, or soil.

End-of-Experiment Rules

46. After an experiment has been completed, turn off all burners or hot plates. If you used a gas burner, check that the gas-line valve to the burner is off. Unplug hot plates.

47. Turn off and unplug any other electrical equipment that you used.

48. Clean up your work area and return all equipment to its proper place.

49. Dispose of waste materials as instructed by your teacher.

50. Wash your hands after every experiment.

Star Charts

Autumn Sky

To use this chart, hold it up in front of you and turn it so that the direction you are facing is at the bottom of the chart. This chart works best at 34° north latitude, but can be used at other times and latitudes within the continental United States. It works best at the following times: 10:00 P.M. on September 1; 9:00 P.M. on September 15; 8:00 P.M. on September 30.

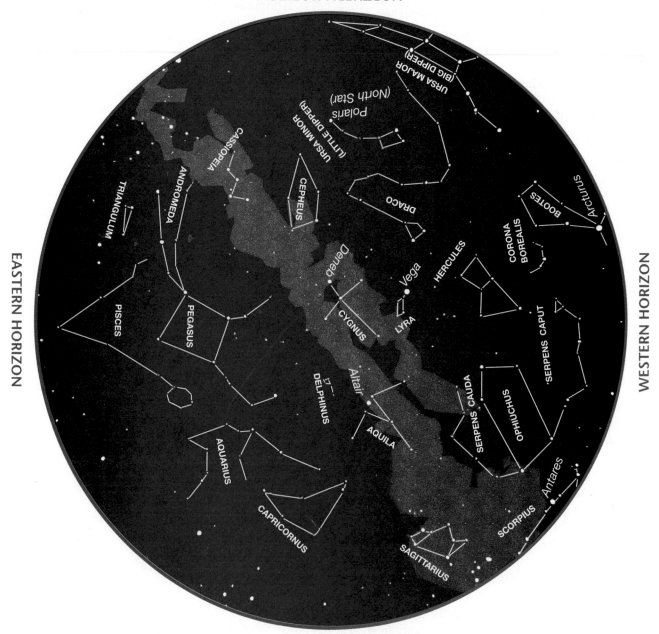

NORTHERN HORIZON

EASTERN HORIZON

WESTERN HORIZON

SOUTHERN HORIZON

Winter Sky

To use this chart, hold it up in front of you and turn it so that the direction you are facing is at the bottom of the chart. This chart works best at 34° north latitude, but can be used at other times and latitudes within the continental United States. It works best at the following times: 10:00 P.M. on December 1; 9:00 P.M. on December 15; 8:00 P.M. on December 30.

Spring Sky

To use this chart, hold it up in front of you and turn it so that the direction you are facing is at the bottom of the chart. This chart works best at 34° north latitude, but can be used at other times and latitudes within the continental United States. It works best at the following times: 10:00 P.M. on March 1; 9:00 P.M. on March 15; 8:00 P.M. on March 30.

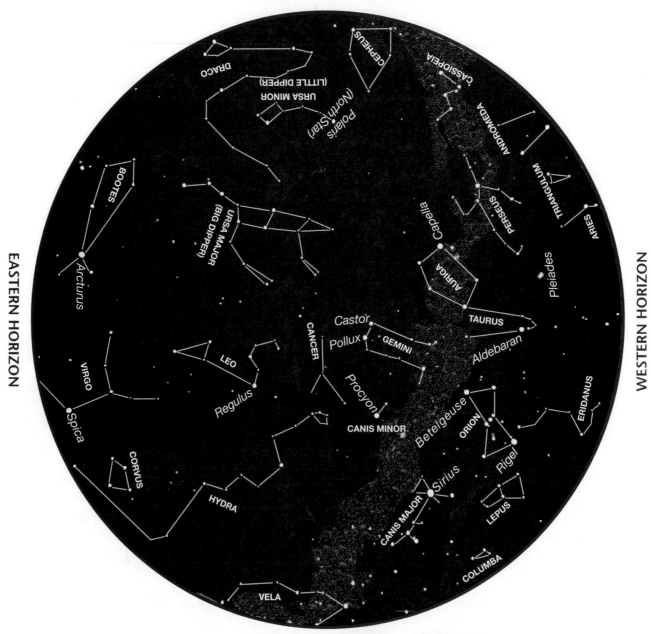

Summer Sky

To use this chart, hold it up in front of you and turn it so that the direction you are facing is at the bottom of the chart. This chart works best at 34° north latitude, but can be used at other times and latitudes within the continental United States. It works best at the following times: 10:00 P.M. on June 1; 9:00 P.M. on June 15; 8:00 P.M. on June 30.

NORTHERN HORIZON

EASTERN HORIZON

WESTERN HORIZON

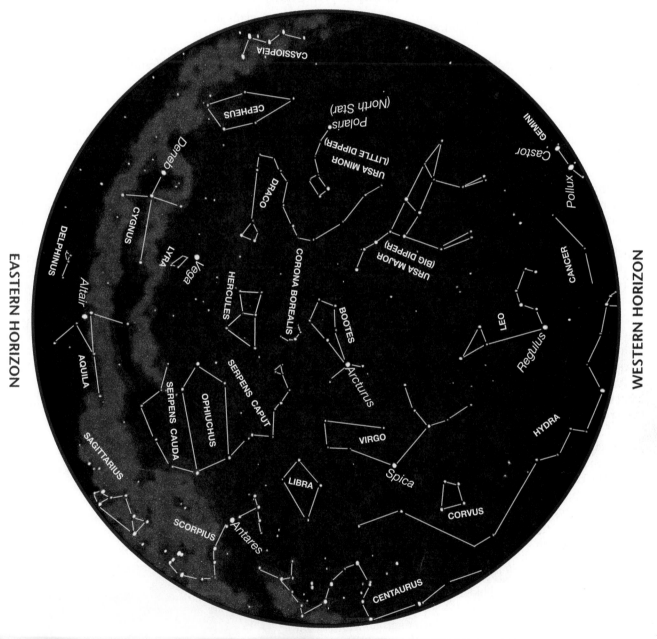

SOUTHERN HORIZON

Glossary

absolute magnitude The brightness of a star if it were a standard distance from Earth. (p. 108)

apparent magnitude The brightness of a star as seen from Earth. (p. 107)

asteroid belt The region of the solar system between the orbits of Mars and Jupiter, where many asteroids are found. (p. 82)

asteroids Objects revolving around the sun that are too small and too numerous to be considered planets. (p. 82)

astronomy The study of the moon, stars, and other objects in space. (p. 15)

autumnal equinox The day of the year that marks the beginning of fall in the Northern Hemisphere. (p. 21)

axis An imaginary line that passes through Earth's center and the North and South poles, about which Earth rotates. (p. 15)

big bang The initial explosion that resulted in the formation and expansion of the universe. (p. 122)

binary star A star system that contains two stars. (p. 117)

black hole The remains of an extremely massive star pulled into a small volume by the force of gravity. (p. 115)

chromosphere The middle layer of the sun's atmosphere. (p. 57)

comet A ball of ice and dust whose orbit is a long, narrow ellipse. (p. 80)

constellation A pattern of stars in the sky. (p. 94)

controlled experiment An experiment in which all factors except one are kept constant. (p. 139)

convex lens A piece of transparent glass curved so that the middle is thicker than the edges. (p. 96)

core The central part of the sun, where nuclear fusion occurs. (p. 56)

corona The outer layer of the sun's atmosphere. (p. 57)

crater A round pit on the moon's surface. (p. 41)

eclipse The partial or total blocking of one object by another. (p. 27)

eclipsing binary A star system in which one star periodically blocks the light from another. (p. 118)

electromagnetic radiation Energy that travels through space in the form of waves. (p. 95)

ellipse An elongated circle, or oval shape; the shape of the planets' orbits. (p. 53)

elliptical galaxy A galaxy shaped like a flattened ball, containing only old stars. (p. 120)

equinox The two days of the year on which neither hemisphere is tilted toward or away from the sun. (p. 21)

extraterrestrial life Life that arises outside of Earth. (p. 84)

galaxy A giant structure that contains hundreds of billions of stars. (p. 103)

gas giants The name given to the first four outer planets: Jupiter, Saturn, Uranus, and Neptune. (p. 70)

geocentric A description of the solar system in which all of the planets revolve around Earth. (p. 51)

geosynchronous orbit The orbit of a satellite that revolves around Earth at the same rate that Earth rotates. (p. 37)

giant star A very large star, much larger than the sun. (p. 106)

gravity The attractive force between two objects; its magnitude depends on their masses and the distance between them. (p. 32)

greenhouse effect The trapping of heat by a planet's atmosphere. (p. 66)

heliocentric A description of the solar system in which all of the planets revolve around the sun. (p. 52)

Hertzsprung-Russell diagram A graph relating the temperature and brightness of stars. (p. 108)

hypothesis A possible explanation for a set of observations or answer to a scientific question; must be testable. (p. 139)

inertia The tendency of a moving object to continue in a straight line or a stationary object to remain in place. (p. 53)

irregular galaxy A galaxy that does not have a regular shape. (p. 120)

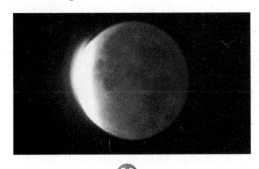

satellite Any object that revolves around another object in space. (p. 36)

solar eclipse The blocking of sunlight to Earth that occurs when the moon is between the sun and Earth. (p. 28)

solar flare An explosion of hydrogen gas from the sun's surface that occurs when loops in sunspot regions suddenly connect. (p. 60)

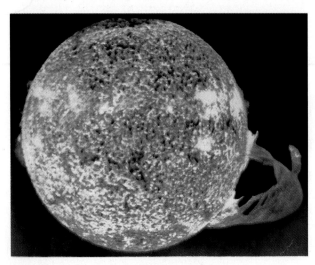

solar wind A stream of electrically charged particles produced by the sun's corona. (p. 58)

solstice The two days of the year on which the noon sun is directly overhead at either 23.5° South or 23.5° North. (p. 20)

spectrograph An instrument that separates light into colors and photographs the resulting spectrum. (p. 99)

spectrum The range of wavelengths of electro-magnetic waves. (p. 95)

spiral galaxy A galaxy whose arms curve outward in a pinwheel pattern. (p. 120)

spring tide A tide with the greatest difference between low and high tides. (p. 33)

sunspot A dark area of gas on the sun that is cooler than surrounding gases. (p. 58)

supernova The explosion of a dying giant or supergiant star. (p. 114)

telescope A device built to study distant objects by making them appear closer. (p. 41)

terrestrial planets The name given to the four inner planets: Mercury, Venus, Earth, and Mars. (p. 62)

tide The rise and fall of the level of water in the ocean. (p. 32)

umbra The darkest part of a shadow. (p. 28)

universe All of space and everything in it. (p. 103)

variable Any factor that can change in an experiment. (p. 139)

vernal equinox The day of the year that marks the beginning of spring in the Northern Hemisphere. (p. 21)

visible light Electromagnetic radiation that can be seen with the unaided eye. (p. 95)

wavelength The distance between the crest of one wave and the crest of the next. (p. 95)

white dwarf The remaining hot core of a star after its outer layers have expanded and drifted out into space. (p. 114)

Acknowledgments

Staff Credits

The people who made up the **Science Explorer** team—representing design services, editorial, editorial services, electronic publishing technology, manufacturing & inventory planning, marketing, marketing services, market research, online services & multimedia development, production services, product planning, project office, and publishing processes—are listed below.

Carolyn Belanger, Barbara A. Bertell, Suzanne Biron, Peggy Bliss, Peter W. Brooks, Christopher R. Brown, Greg Cantone, Jonathan Cheney, Todd Christy, Lisa J. Clark, Patrick Finbarr Connolly, Edward Cordero, Robert Craton, Patricia Cully, Patricia M. Dambry, Kathleen J. Dempsey, Judy Elgin, Gayle Connolly Fedele, Frederick Fellows, Barbara Foster, Paula Foye, Loree Franz, Donald P. Gagnon Jr., Paul J. Gagnon, Joel Gendler, Elizabeth Good, Robert M. Graham, Kerri Hoar, Joanne Hudson, Linda D. Johnson, Anne Jones, Toby Klang, Carolyn Langley, Russ Lappa, Carolyn Lock, Cheryl Mahan, Dotti Marshall, Meredith Mascola, Jeanne Y. Maurand, Karen McHugh, Eve Melnechuk, Natania Mlawer, Paul W. Murphy, Cindy A. Noftle, Julia F. Osborne, Judi Pinkham, Caroline M. Power, Robin L. Santel, Suzanne J. Schineller, Emily Soltanoff, Kira Thaler-Marbit, Mark Tricca, Diane Walsh, Pearl Weinstein, Merce Wilczek, Helen Young.

Illustration

John Edwards & Associates: 19, 25, 26, 28, 29, 33, 54–55, 63t, 71, 82, 106, 115, 118, 119, 122b, 123
Martucci Design: 61, 95b, 100, 112
Jared D. Lee: 104
Morgan Cain & Associates: 15, 18, 22, 27, 35, 36, 37, 47, 59, 63, 75, 81, 91, 101, 105, 109, 111, 122t, 127, 132
Matt Mayerchak: 45, 125
Ortelius Design Inc.: 16, 17
J/B Woolsey Associates: 95t, 96

Photography

Photo Research Kerri Hoar, PoYee McKenna Oster
Cover Image NASA

Nature of Science
Page 8t, Digital Vision; **8b,** Jane Luu; **8b background,** David Jewitt and Jane Luu; **9tr, br,** Jet Propulsion Laboratory; **9mr,** Digital Vision; **10,** John Sanford/Astrostock Art Resource.

Chapter 1
Pages 12–13, NASA; **14t,** Russ Lappa; **14b,** Eric Lessing; **16t,** Corel Corp.; **16b,** Archive Photos; **17t,** Courtney Milne/Masterfile; **17b,** Hazel Hankin/Stock Boston; **20,** Palmer/Kane/TSI; **21,** Art Wolfe/TSI; **23,** Richard Haynes; **24t,** Richard Haynes; **24b,** Larry Landolfi/Photo Researchers; **26mr,** Jerry Lodriguss/Photo Researchers; **26tl, ml, bl, tm, bm, tr, br,** John Bova/Photo Researchers; **28, 29tr, 29br,** Jay M. Pasachoff; **31,** Richard Haynes; **both,** Nancy Dudley/Stock Boston; **34,** Jim Zipp/Photo Researchers; **35t,** Richard Haynes; **36–38,** NASA; **39t,** Richard Haynes; **39b,** NASA; **40t,** John Bova/Photo Researchers; **40b all,** Alastair G.W. Cameron/Harvard-Smithsonian Center for Astrophysics; **41tl,** NASA; **41br,** Jay M. Pasachoff; **42,** N. Armstrong/The Stock Market; **43,** TSI; **44,** NASA.

Chapter 2
Pages 48–49, NASA; **50t,** Russ Lappa; **50b,** Anglo-Australian Observatory, photograph by David Malin; **51–53b,** The Granger Collection, NY; **53t,** Richard Haynes; **57,** Digital Vision; **58,** National Solar Observatory; **58 inset, 60t,** Space Telescope Science Institute; **60b,** National Solar Observatory; **64r,** NASA; **64 inset,** A.S.P./Science Source/Photo Researchers; **65–66,** Digital Vision; **67,** NASA; **68,** Jet Propulsion Laboratory; **69 both,** NASA; **70,** TSI; **72 both,** NASA; **73, 74tr,** Jet Propulsion Laboratory; **74 inset,** Digital Vision; **74b, 75, 76 both, 77,** NASA; **78–80t,** Richard Haynes; **80b,** Space Telescope Science Institute; **82tr,** Jet Propulsion Laboratory; **83tl,** U. S. Geological Survey; **83tr,** Jerry Schad/Photo Researchers; **84,** Ghislaine Grozaz; **85,** James Pisarowicz; **86,** U. S. Geological Survey; **87,** NASA; **88–89,** Jet Propulsion Laboratory.

Chapter 3
Pages 92–93, David Nunuk/Science Photo Library/Photo Researchers; **94t,** Richard Haynes; **94b,** John Sanford/Science Photo Library/Photo Researchers; **96,** Russ Lappa; **97t,** Malin/Pasachoff/Caltech 1992; **97b,** NRAO/Science Photo Library/Photo Researchers; **98tl,** Yerkes Observatory; **98–99tr,** National Astronomy and Ionosphere Center; **98–99br,** John Sanford/Astrostock; **99tr,** NASA; **102,** Silver, Burdett & Ginn Publishing; **103t,** Richard Haynes; **103b,** Roger Harris/Science Photo Library/Photo Researchers; **106 inset,** UCO/Lick Observatory photo/image; **107,** Luke Dodd/Science Photo library/Photo Researchers; **108,** Anglo-Australian Observatory, photograph by David Malin; **112b,** Open University, UK; **113tr,** National Optical Astronomy Observatories; **113br,** Space Telescope Science Institute; **114, 116,** Photo Researchers; **117,** Dennis Di Cicco/Peter Arnold; **118 both,** Richard Haynes; **120t, 120m,** Anglo-Australian Observatory, photograph by David Malin; **120b,** Royal Observatory, Edinburgh/AATB/Science Photo Library/Photo Researchers; **121,** NASA; **124,** David Parker/Science Photo Library/Photo Researchers.

Interdisciplinary Exploration
Page 128t, Jet Propulsion Laboratory; **128b,** U. S. Geological Survey; **129r,** Valerie Ambroise; **129l,** Corbis-Bettmann; **130t,** Pat Rawlings/NASA; **130–131b,** Jet Propulsion Laboratory; **131tr, 131tl,** NASA; **132t,** U. S. Geological Survey; **132b,** NASA/Peter Arnold; **133,** Pat Rawlings/NASA.

Skills Handbook
Page 134, Mike Moreland/Photo Network; **135t,** Foodpix; **135m,** Richard Haynes; **135b,** Russ Lappa; **138,** Richard Haynes; **140,** Ron Kimball; **141,** Renee Lynn/Photo Researchers.

Appendix B
Pages 150–153, Griffith Observer, Griffith Observatory, Los Angeles.